THE BUSY PERSON'S GUIDE TO PRAYER

DEACON GREG KANDRA

the WORD among us® press

Published by The Word Among Us Press
7115 Guilford Drive, Suite 100
Frederick, Maryland 21704
wau.org

24 23 22 21 20   2 3 4 5 6

ISBN: 978-1-59325-351-6
eISBN: 978-1-59325-525-1

Nihil Obstat: Msgr. Michael Morgan, J.D., J.C.L.
Censor Librorum
February 6, 2019

Imprimatur: +Most Rev. Felipe J. Estévez, S.T.D.
Diocese of St. Augustine
February 6, 2019

"You've Got a Friend in Me: The Prayer of Friendship" is expanded from an essay that originally appeared in the March 17, 2003 issue of *America* magazine.

Cover design by Faceout Studios

Made and printed in the United States of America

Library of Congress Control Number: 2019933003

PRAISE FOR *THE BUSY PERSON'S GUIDE TO PRAYER*

"With countless priorities pulling at us, connecting with God can seem like one more obligation to squeeze in to our schedule. Deacon Greg—self-described as a writer, journalist, blogger, storyteller, preacher, husband, and deacon—gives us a book that helps us to remember why we pray, how 'shockingly simple' prayer should be, and how to maintain a habit of prayer. With plenty of tips and examples, Deacon Greg is a friend on your journey to connect with God, and bring peace to your days. Don't let this treasure pass you by."
—**Bishop Robert Reed,** The CatholicTV Network

"Deacon Greg has long been one of my favorite spiritual writers, and this book only affirms that. His guidance on prayer is wise, clear, and down-to-earth. It's for people who, like him, live in the noisy, busy world—stressful day jobs, cabs and subways, phones and distractions. It's a guide to ordinary holiness. You don't need to join a monastery to become a master at prayer. This great book opens that possibility for anyone."
—**Brandon Vogt,** founder of ClaritasU and author of *Why I Am Catholic*

"As a veteran journalist Greg Kandra has amply demonstrated how well he can find a meaningful story in small moments that others might miss. As a Catholic deacon, he teaches us how to notice such moments, too, and then make the most of them through prayer, so we may learn about God, ourselves, and the world around us. My first prayer after reading this book was

one of gratitude that so gifted a storyteller as Deacon Greg Kandra took the time to teach us how to 'take time for prayer.'"
—**Elizabeth Scalia,** editor-at-large of Word on Fire Catholic Ministries and author of *Little Sins Mean a Lot*

"Deacon Greg Kandra, award winning journalist, has become one of the Church's finest spiritual writers, and this wonderful book illustrates why. While he writes in a simple conversational style, his insights and suggestions on prayer are profound. In today's tumultuous world, Deacon Greg offers what we all need: a voice of calm spiritual maturity reminding us of the direct, simple and loving relationship we have with God. This little book will become a spiritual classic, as Deacon Kandra calls us to consider, to try, and to pray."
—**Deacon William T. Ditewig,** PhD, former executive director of the Secretariat for the Diaconate at the United States Conference of Catholic Bishops

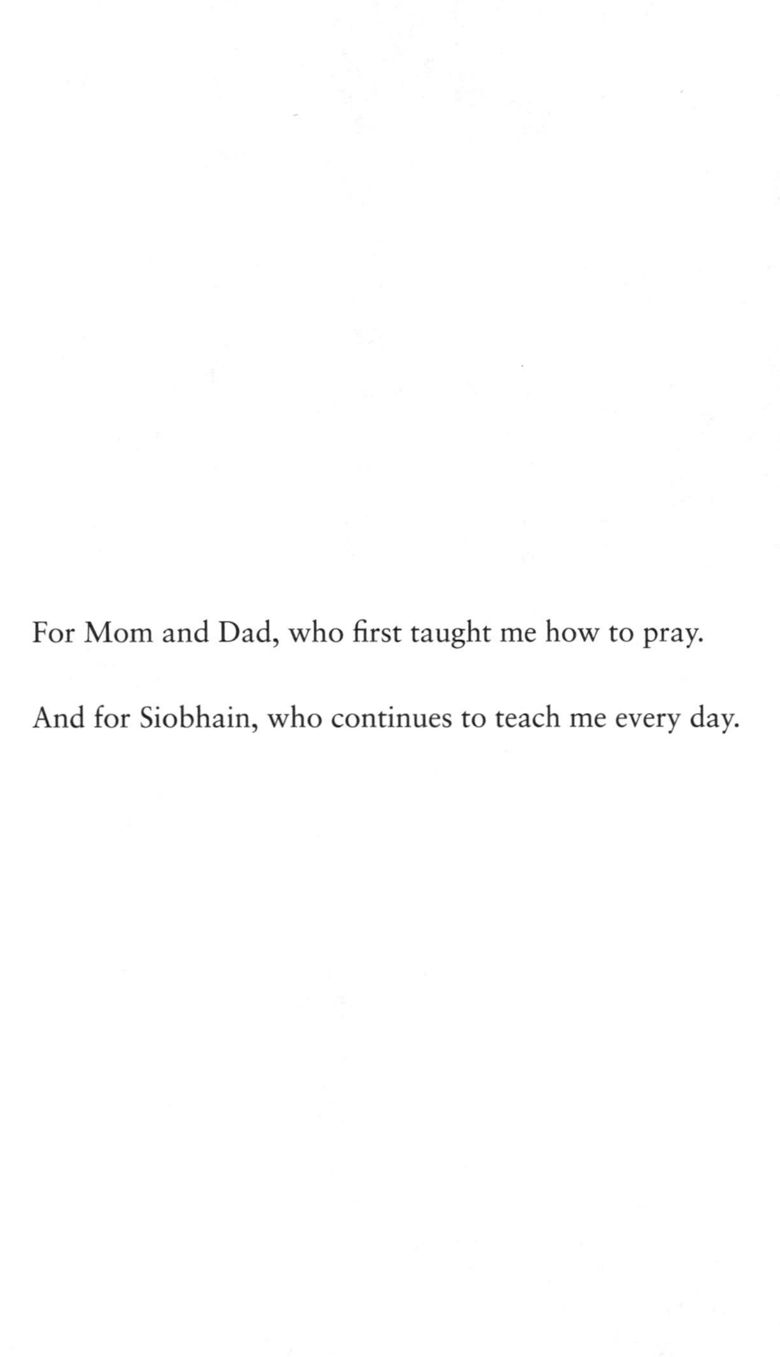

For Mom and Dad, who first taught me how to pray.

And for Siobhain, who continues to teach me every day.

CONTENTS

INTRODUCTION

One of my earliest memories is of something I never want to forget: my mother teaching me to pray.

I was three or four years old, and it was still early evening when my mother tucked me into bed in my room, in our house on Morgal Street, Rockville, Maryland. She whispered, "Say your prayers. You know how to pray? You do it like this":

> Angel of God, my guardian dear,
> To whom God's love commits me here,
> Ever this day, be at my side
> To light, to guard, to rule, to guide.
> Amen.

And that was how it began.

Now, nearly sixty years later, I look back on that time and it seems so simple. Life was simple, yes. But so was praying. There's a plainness and purity to that prayer, with all those short, easy words and the unabashedly humble request: *Guardian Angel, take care of me. G'night.*

As I got older, prayer became more challenging—the Our Father, Hail Mary, Glory Be, then the Memorare and assorted chaplets, and then the Rosary, the Creed, the Prayer of St.

Francis, and on and on and on. Oh, the Rosary! How I remember the May Procession at St. Peter's Catholic School, walking around in the May sun, reciting decade after decade, and the ancient and grim-faced Sister Irenaeus, swathed in black, pummeling the organ as we sang "Immaculate Mary" and "Hail, Holy Queen." Did praying have to be that hard? And hot? Did it have to be done in the heat?

Many years later, when I was ordained as a deacon, I discovered the Liturgy of the Hours and praying the psalms, the Magnificat, and Benedictus.

These are all part of the glorious legacy of the Church, and every Catholic should be familiar with them. But not everyone has the inclination—or, significantly, the time—to pray.

And there's the rub.

Let's face it: in a world where soccer practice, work, the gym, PTA meetings, school projects, Twitter, and Netflix dominate our lives, it can be challenging and seemingly impossible to find time to pray. There are deadlines to meet, bills to pay, babies to diaper, reports to file, gardens to weed, emails to answer, groceries to buy. And praying? Talking to God? Amid the stresses and strains of daily life, many of us take God's name in vain, if we mention him at all.

We want to pray, but who has the time?

Well . . . you. *You* do. Yes, you. The busy person who can't find your keys or this week's grocery list can, in fact, find time to pray. It is *not* impossible. If you're reading this right now, you want to know how you can do what you feel called to do, what you *want* to do, but that you somehow can't find the *opportunity* to do: pray. To offer up a good word to our good God. To stay connected to the Creator in a way that is fruitful and intimate and will nourish the soul—and just maybe do some good.

How can I do that? you're wondering.

Glad you asked.

This little book is intended to offer a plan of action—a way to pray when you feel you just can't. (Yes, you *can*. Really.) Building a steady and fulfilling prayer life can be done, even if you think it can't.

But be forewarned: I offer here no magic formulas, no easy solutions. This isn't like one of those diets where you can "sleep" the pounds away. You will have to do some work. But as St. Benedict put it when he wrote his famous Rule, I'm hoping this won't be "harsh or burdensome."

To that end, I'll be providing helpful handrails along the way to guide us on this journey. Each chapter concludes with some thoughts on prayer from people you know by faith (saints and popes, for example) and people you may not know—friends and acquaintances of mine who offer their own words of wisdom on the subject of prayer. I've also included some action items to get your prayer muscles in shape, and a brief prayer of my own to help put into words what we are trying to do.

THE BEST PRAYER IS AN ACT OF LOVE. AT ITS ROOT, IT REALLY SHOULD BE DECEPTIVELY, ALMOST SHOCKINGLY, SIMPLE.

I don't intend to ladle out heavy theology or philosophy; I'm not going to be quoting exhaustively from encyclicals or treatises; I won't be dissecting the mind of Aquinas. That's not me. I'm just a writer, journalist, blogger, storyteller, preacher, husband, and deacon.

And I'm a busy person who is still trying to make time to pray.

It isn't easy. Believe me, I know.

But this book, I hope, will offer some ideas on how to get started.

The best prayer is an act of boundless surrender and joy, communicating with God in a way that is unique, intimate, and utterly honest. It is an act of love. And at its root, it really should be deceptively, almost shockingly, simple.

"Angel of God, my Guardian dear . . ."

Yes, that simple.

I hope you'll find this to be a helpful handbook that will encourage more prayer—a paperback stepping-stone that will, as a famous prayer to the Holy Spirit puts it, "Enkindle . . . the fire of God's love."

Ready to strike a match and start the flame?

Then let us pray.

CHAPTER 1

WHY AM I DOING THIS?

Persevere in prayer, being watchful in it
with thanksgiving.
—Colossians 4:2

Let me begin these thoughts on prayer where a lot of us begin the act of praying: in church.

One of my favorite places to go to get away from it all is the legendary Abbey of Gethsemani, the celebrated Trappist monastery in Kentucky made famous by Thomas Merton. It is a mecca for "Mertonites"—I confess I'm one—and offers ample opportunities for praying, bird-watching, napping, and eating (try the fruitcake or the fudge!).

Like a lot of people there on retreat, whenever I visit, I spend a significant amount of time in the abbey church, praying the psalms with the monks and watching the light from the windows dapple the plain white walls. The church has a vast, empty feel to it, and I suspect many visitors find its plainness boring.

But listen hard enough, and between the psalms and the silence, you can hear the walls speak.

They speak, quite simply, of incompleteness. I think it was meant to be that way.

The abbey church at Gethsemani is probably the world's starkest example of Cistercian architecture—architecture that is the very essence of simplicity. There is supposed to be nothing unnecessary adorning the church—a reminder of monasticism's ancient beginnings in the desert. There are no distractions, few details. The

Kentucky church is all whitewashed walls, plain wooden beams, and pebbled floors. This seems appropriate to the local landscape too. It looks, perhaps intentionally, like an empty tobacco barn you might find in the neighboring hills.

It is a place of texture, as if meant to be touched. But what exactly are we touching? The church suggests more of a rough outline rather than a final draft; it seems somehow unfinished, as if a lot of the work was left undone. No statues? No shrines? No decoration? When will the workers be back to finish the job?

But that, I think, is the point.

Gazing up at the soaring ceiling and the sturdy beams lending their support, you realize that the workers are actually *there*, every day, in the choir and the balcony, as they have been for decade after decade, filling the space with prayer.

To look at that abbey church is to look at a work in progress, filled with people who are *themselves* works in progress. Monks and visitors alike—we are imperfect and unfinished. And in the daily chanting of the psalms, we somehow struggle to refine ourselves and our world. We are finishing the work begun by God.

That is what prayer is all about.

We somehow engage ourselves in the work of completing what God started by raising our voices, hearts, and minds toward the One who started it all. Do we ever really finish? Not really. Like that church, there is always more to do.

And so it is with prayer.

WHY AM I DOING THIS?

Praising, Asking, Thanking

Before we dig in to the task at hand and think more intently and purposefully about the great act of prayer, it helps to ask ourselves a very simple question: why? Why do we pray? Why are we doing this? What do we hope to achieve?

To my way of thinking, you can have many personal reasons for praying, but prayer basically boils down to three things: praise, petition, and thanksgiving. More often than not, when we hit the ground on our knees to have a word with God, it's for one of those three reasons.

Praise is something you find often in the great prayer compendium of David, otherwise known as the Book of Psalms. The ancients were forever singing of God's glorious achievements and extolling his virtues.

> I will praise you, LORD, with all my heart;
> I will declare all your wondrous deeds.
> I will delight and rejoice in you;
> I will sing hymns to your name, Most High. (Psalm 9:2-3)

In our prayers of praise, we let God know that, whether we like it or not, he's in charge. (I know that's a hard pill for some of us to swallow.) We place ourselves before him with trust and hope. We remind ourselves that he is the Creator and we are the created. We marvel at what he has done and wonder at what he may have in store.

In a prayer of **petition,** we come before the Lord to—in effect—ask him for a favor. Well, maybe more than a favor. Maybe, say, a really big, life-changing, world-altering act of generosity and grace. Maybe, even, a miracle.

Our petitions can range from the seemingly trivial to the soul-crushingly urgent, from "Please, Lord, give me good weather on my wedding day" to "Dear God, please let the lab results come back negative." Sometimes, out of desperation and the desire for a miracle, we might try bartering with the Almighty: "Help me pass this test, and I swear I'll never smoke pot again . . ." We may also pray for those we love: "Please heal my mother's sickness . . . take away my daughter's loneliness . . . fix my neighbor's broken marriage . . ."

But frankly, the most beautiful way to offer a prayer of petition is simply to pray, not for what *we* want, but for what *God* wants. It is to place ourselves trustingly in his hands and say, "Thy will be done." We should pray that we can accept whatever that will might be. We see the most powerful and self-sacrificing form of that prayer in Mary's response to Gabriel at the Annunciation: "May it be done to me according to your word" (Luke 1:38).

WE ARE ALL WORKS IN PROGRESS, PRAYING THAT GOD BRINGS US TO COMPLETION.

How many of us have been able to say *that* to God? If you want to talk about a work in progress, consider how much work most of us have to do to even come close to that kind of surrender, fidelity, trustfulness, and love.

To be able to do that, I think, is to approach the serenity of the saints.

Finally, there is the prayer of **thanksgiving.** When I was growing up, my mother always made the writing thank-you notes a priority during the holidays. Before the wrapping paper was in the trash and the needles had begun to fall off the tree, we had to write those notes and get them in the mail.

All of which makes me wonder: could we do any less for God?

So often we come to God with a pleading attitude of "gimme, gimme, gimme." We ask, we implore, we plead, we bargain, we promise. But how often do we bring that same sense of urgency to whispering a humble "thank you" to God? How often do we thank him for his patience in listening to us? How often do we thank him for what he has already given us, not merely the things we continually want?

Hearts Full of Hope

The beautiful reality is this: God never tires of giving us what we need, though it may not be what we want. Every prayer is answered, though it may not be answered the way we would prefer.

But with hearts full of hope, we cannot fail to extend to God our gratitude and our thanksgiving for his attention, his goodness, his tender compassion, his love.

One result is that prayer gently, subtly, and tenderly brings about change—if not in our world, then in us and in how we perceive that world. The act of praying can work wonders on our attitude, our state of mind, and our state of heart. It truly can help bring about peace.

Dr. Andrew Newburg, of Philadelphia's Thomas Jefferson Hospital, has studied the positive impact of prayer on the human body. He told *NBC News* that prayer has a distinct and mysterious ability to change us: "You become connected to God. You become connected to the world. Your self sort of goes away."[1]

The *Catechism of the Catholic Church* puts it this way:

> If our prayer is resolutely united with that of Jesus, in trust and boldness as children, we obtain all that we ask in his name, even more than any particular thing: the Holy Spirit himself, who contains all gifts. (2741)

This is another way of saying that prayer doesn't necessarily give us what we want, but it supplies what we need: God's Spirit and his abundant grace.

It helps to remember that the changes brought about by prayer may not happen overnight. Like that magnificently stark church in Kentucky, we are all works in progress, praying that God brings us to completion.

Indeed, the act of prayer is the hammer and nail of the work we undertake—tools for erecting a life that is not only whole but holy.

Prayer is putting oneself in the hands of God, at His disposition, and listening to His voice in the depth of our hearts.

—St. Teresa of Calcutta[2]

God knows what's in our hearts. Keeping that top of mind, I maintain a conversation with the Lord throughout the day in addition to my usual devotions. I share joyful moments with him in thanksgiving, and I ask for strength when the weight of my concerns bears heavily in my heart. I also very frequently beg his mercy when I fall short of doing right by my call to be his child.

In the commotion of the morning push to get the kids ready for school, in the excitement of completing a project in the office, in the slow drive home, in the silence beside my wife at night before sleeping, he is with me and knows what's in my heart.

—Jonas Geronimo, husband and father,
Anaheim, California

Before taking time to pray, it's good to ask yourself, "What do I really hope to say to God? What do I need *him* to say to *me?* Why does praying at this moment, in this place, matter to me?"

Many (maybe most) times, we may not know the answer. But something compels us to reach out to God in praise, in petition, or in thanksgiving—or even in all three.

Take a moment at the start of every prayer to remind yourself that God is ready to listen to whatever you have to say. And then, as a familiar saying puts it, "Let go and let God." The One who made you knows what makes you tick. Trust him. Trust your heart. And give him that moment.

You may be surprised what you get in return.

Dear God,

This is hard.

Words do not come to me. My heart is confused.

I'm crowded with thoughts, ideas,

insecurities, hopes, dreams.

Life is crazy. I don't know where to begin.

So let's just begin. Okay?

I'm here. I love you. I know you love me.

I trust you to guide me where you need me to be.

Where I need to be, right now, is closer to you.

Can you help me make that so?

I'm trying to make you a bigger and better part of my life.

Can you help me make that so?

I'm trying to be better to others,

better to myself,

better to my friends and family,

and even to the annoying people I don't really like very much.

I'm trying. And failing. And trying.

I'm really trying to be the person you want me to be.

Can you help make that so?

I believe you can. I believe you will.

I believe.

Truly.

I believe.
Take that belief, dear God, and take all that I am
and make of it all something beautiful
and bold
and brave.
Maybe, even, something holy.
This is hard.
But I know you will make it easier.
Let's do this.
Please?
Thank you.
Amen.

CHAPTER 2

GETTING STARTED

Let the words of my mouth be acceptable,
the thoughts of my heart before you,
LORD, my rock and my redeemer.
—Psalm 19:15

One summer afternoon, I found myself in a small Vietnamese restaurant in Midtown Manhattan, sharing a table for lunch with a couple of other people—one of them, a bishop from India. He was from the northern part of the country, a place where most of the people are farmers or fishermen and, by and large, poor. They travel on foot, if they travel at all, though some might have bicycles or own livestock they can hitch to a cart.

Significantly, it is a place where many people have never heard the name "Jesus."

This is no small thing; it is the very definition of what you might call "mission country." There are few priests, brothers, or sisters. The bishop has no fancy home. He has no budget, no big office, no staff, no cathedral. He spends much of his time traveling around the diocese, visiting different missions, often sleeping on the floor.

With few religious to serve this flock, most of those who minister to the faithful are laypeople—catechists who lead prayer services, tell Bible stories, or teach.

They are ready to spread the gospel however they can, wherever they can, using whatever means they can, often at great risk. They live every day with the very real threat of martyrdom.

"I tell them," the bishop said over lunch, "at maximum you may lose your head. Get ready for it! And they respond, 'We are ready!'"

Yet these courageous people do what they do anyway, in the face of daunting challenges, with love, zeal, and unwavering, unshakable faith.

In most places, Mass is not celebrated very often, but when it is, the people make the most of it. Sometimes they'll spend half a day walking to a village to attend Mass and then spend the other half of the day walking home, joyfully celebrating the simple fact that they were able to hear the gospel proclaimed, receive the Body of Christ, go to Confession, or ask the priest to bless their children.

The bishop described one woman who attended Mass whenever she could, however she could. She was not yet baptized, so she was unable to receive the Eucharist. She went to church—a makeshift affair outdoors, with plain wooden benches and a humble altar—and saw her friends and neighbors receiving Communion, yet she could not. This made her sad. This woman not only yearned for Christ—she literally hungered for him.

And so she did what she felt was the next best thing to actually receiving the Eucharist. At every Mass, she kept her eye on a person going up for Communion, looked to see where they were sitting, and then moved to sit next to them in the pew.

In her heart, she said to herself, "Jesus is here. I want to be as close to him as I can." This was her Communion.

What love for the Lord! And what love for the Body of Christ.

This was her greatest joy.

It should be ours too.

We all desire to be that close to the Lord. We hunger to draw near and want to do whatever we can to make that closeness a reality. This desire is rooted within each of us, in our longing to be intimate with the One who made us and imagined us into being.

It is a desire whose deepest expression begins, of course, with prayer.

Prayer itself needs to begin with a kind of desire as well—the unmistakable tug of the heart that tells us quietly, insistently, "Try this. Go ahead. Pray."

You wouldn't be reading this if you didn't have that desire already, right?

The *Catechism* says,

> Where does prayer come from? Whether prayer is expressed in words or gestures, it is the whole man who prays. But in naming the source of prayer, Scripture speaks sometimes of the soul or the spirit, but most often of the heart (more than a thousand times). According to Scripture, it is the *heart* that prays. (2562)

The heart is where prayer has to begin.

Always in His Presence

Years ago, Thomas Merton was walking the streets of New York with a Jewish friend. It was just a few months after his conversion and Baptism. Now that Merton was a Catholic, his friend reasoned, he should want to be the best Catholic possible. His friend explained that from his perspective as an observant Jew, the most important thing a Christian should want is to become a saint.

Merton stopped him. "But how do I do that?"

His friend replied very simply, "You become a saint, first and foremost, by wanting it."

Similarly, we begin to have a prayer life, first and foremost, by *wanting* it.

We seek a way to talk with God because the desire burns in our heart and we want to draw closer to him—and have him draw closer to us. Like the woman in India, we need to find communion with the Lord, however we can do it, even if means just sitting next to him on a rickety wooden bench.

One way to begin any prayerful effort is by acknowledging that simple desire: the hunger for him.

In my experience, it is not uncommon for someone to begin a church meeting or prayer group gathering by saying solemnly, "Let's take a moment to place ourselves in the presence of God." That has always struck me as fundamentally off-kilter and more than a little bit wrong; we don't need to *place ourselves* in his presence, because we are *already* in his presence.

WE BEGIN TO HAVE A PRAYER LIFE, FIRST AND FOREMOST, BY *WANTING* IT.

I have a wooden plaque in my office that puts it succinctly: "Bidden or not bidden, God is present."

Know this—and it's something most of us learn when we are children but easily forget as we mature—God is everywhere.

Every prayer should begin not with us orienting ourselves toward God, but with us acknowledging that God has *already* oriented himself toward us. The name of the Messiah, let us remember, is Emmanuel, "God with us." He is never far from us.

Truth be told, more often than not, we are the ones who are far from him.

Prayer expresses our desire to get as close as we can.

But how do we do that in a practical way?

For many Catholics, every prayer begins with the most basic gesture of piety we know, the Sign of the Cross. With this sign, we reenact our Baptism and state that what we are about to do is done in the name of the Trinity.

But after that?

Jesus offers his followers this advice: "When you pray, go to your inner room, close the door, and pray to your Father in secret. And your Father who sees in secret will repay you" (Matthew 6:6). He leaves it to our imagination to decide what constitutes "your inner room"—a location that may not necessarily be geographic or the sort of "man cave" frequently mentioned on HGTV's *House Hunters*.

The inner room is a mental and spiritual place that is secluded, set apart. It is hidden from the world. Finding it in our own busy age can be a challenge. Try this: carve out five minutes of your day. Find a quiet, out-of-the-way corner of your world—it could even be the bathroom, the garage, or the laundry room—and dedicate those five minutes in that particular space to clearing your head, stilling your thoughts, and beginning to talk to God. Unsure how to start? Make the Sign of the Cross. Take a deep breath. And tell God what is on your mind.

The Liturgy of the Hours begins with this simple plea: "God, come to my assistance. Lord, make haste to help me." I find that this appeal to God gets my mind working, and it sends up a signal flare to the Almighty: "I'm here. Let's talk."

Go ahead. Try it.

Be still. Be alert. Be ready.

Then begin.

> For me, prayer is a surge of the heart;
> it is a simple look turned toward heaven, it is a cry
> of recognition and of love, embracing both trial and joy.
>
> —St. Thérèse of Lisieux[3]

I don't always find peace in my daily prayer. In fact, sometimes it's a struggle. But I know that a marriage is formed in the daily decision to love your spouse, and in a similar way, when I decided to pray every single day, no matter how I felt, my heart started to change. It wasn't so much about what I could get out of it, but what it means to be with God. Prayer changed me.

—Marcel LeJeune, president and founder of Catholic Missionary Disciples, College Station, Texas

Remember: God is not a distant figure, remote or detached. He's closer than you think. Imagine that he is not only near you, not only in the same room with you, but sitting right beside you. He sees what you see, hears what you hear. Hold on to that. Maybe he's beside you on the subway or behind you on the bus.

He's waiting to hear from you. Take a few minutes, find a secluded corner, seek out quiet—and then seek out God. How would you begin to talk with him? What would you want to say to break the ice? Just open your heart—and speak.

Dear God,
I trust you are here.
Help me to be here for you.
Help me to share with you what is in my heart.
In the busyness of my life,
in the craziness of my days,
in the whirlwind of deadlines and pressures
and the stress of never having enough minutes or hours . . .
Help me to be still.
Help me to be calm.
Help me to be nothing more and nothing less than your child.
I am here today to tell you that I love you.
You know my strengths and weaknesses, my sorrows and my joys.
Know, too, that in spite of everything,
though I may not often say it,
I love you.
I trust and hope in your love for me.
Be my guide as I struggle through the frenzy of life . . .
the work I fear I won't finish;
the projects I worry I won't complete;
the expectations I wonder if I'll ever meet.
Though I can't always find the words or the time to give you what you deserve,

I believe you always give me what I need.

In you I place my trust . . .

For you, I offer my days . . .

With you, I know I can do anything.

Thank you for that, and for so much more.

I need you to know all these things (as if you didn't know everything already!).

Stay with me, and be my guide, my hope, my help, my strength.

Please.

Thank you.

Amen.

CHAPTER 3

KEEPING IT SIMPLE

"In praying, do not babble like the pagans, who think that they will be heard because of their many words. Do not be like them. Your Father knows what you need before you ask him."

—Matthew 6:7-8

What if you had only a minute to give to God?

Suppose you had just sixty seconds to tell him what was on your mind. What would you say? What would you want him to know? You don't have time to be flowery. No time to elaborate or explain. Just spit it out. How would you cut to the chase?

Well, here's an idea. Start by taking a page from the Gospel According to Luke. Luke tells of a blind man who was able to get the attention of Jesus one day. Jesus, ever the pragmatist, is disarmingly blunt: "What do you want me to do for you?" (Luke 18:41).

The man replies in the simplest, most direct way imaginable: "Lord, please let me see" (Luke 18:41).

There you have it. If you are wondering how to begin to pray, how to express what is in your heart, how to express what seems inexpressible, look no further. This is how it is done. The blind man expressing his deepest desire—"Lord, please let me see"—is each of us expressing our own pleadings.

Lord, help me understand.

Lord, please calm my anxiety.

Lord, please make what is wrong, right.

Please let me see.

It is a fervent prayer of petition, and it is strikingly, even stunningly, down-to-earth. It also gets results. Jesus acknowledges the blind man's faith and heals him.

So, my first advice to any busy person seeking to find time to pray is just this basic: keep it simple.

We sometimes think we need to offer lengthy prayers from leather-bound books (maybe even in Latin) in order for God to really hear us. We need smoke and beads, chants and responses. Well, no. Not necessarily.

Whether you realize it or not, you already know how to pray. Really. Don't make it more complicated. It is in your bones.

Keep it simple!

St. Teresa of Avila said that prayer should be like a conversation with a friend who knows you even better than you know yourself. How many of us think of prayer that way? How many of us see God as good company on the journey through life?

We don't go to a friend only when we *want* something—to get a lift across town when the car is being fixed, to ask a favor, or maybe to borrow the weed whacker.

We go to a friend for companionship, for joy, for comfort, for affirmation, and for love.

We go to our friends because they enrich us and challenge us. And we want to give to them some of what they give to us. They share our hardships with us, and our joys, and they make us laugh. They enable us to be our best selves—and they are often people who are the most like us. We feel a connection, like they are kindred spirits. We like the same food, cheer the same teams, and have the same anxieties and hopes.

And when we communicate with a friend, it is unvarnished, and honest, and heartfelt, and true. It is fundamentally simple.

That is just as it should be with God.

Our relationship with God, after all, is the ultimate friendship.

Got a Minute?

But how to begin?

As I said at the start: keep it simple. Start with a prayer that is short, familiar, direct. The Lord's Prayer is a good beginning—after all, it's what Jesus taught his disciples when they wanted to learn how to pray. For many of us, it's one of the first prayers we learn.

Or, if you need reassurance, consider these words from Psalm 138: "The Lord is with me to the end. . . . Never forsake the work of your hands" (verse 8).

I think that may be as profound a prayer as you can find: "Never forsake the work of your hands."

It says, "God you have created me. You formed me with your hands. Do not forget me."

Remember me. Stay with me. Please! Give me what you know I need!

It doesn't get any simpler than that.

WHETHER YOU REALIZE IT OR NOT, YOU ALREADY KNOW HOW TO PRAY. REALLY. DON'T MAKE IT MORE COMPLICATED. IT IS IN YOUR BONES.

God doesn't ask of us what we cannot give. If you don't have sixty minutes to offer a litany of prayers, take sixty seconds to pray what is in your heart.

Keep it simple.

And don't be afraid that it isn't enough.

Whether or not we feel like we "get" God or "get" prayer, know this: God "gets" us. Not only does he get us because he made us; he gets us because he *became* us. When he took on human flesh in the form of Jesus, he took on thirty-three years of struggles, stumbles, hunger, and hurts.

God walked the streets of Nazareth, hiked the hillside of Galilee, felt the splash of water from the sea, knew the cold of winter, and the heat of summer, and the crush of the crowds in Jerusalem. He knows what it means to be a busy person with dirt under his nails and sweat on his brow, and too little time to do anything but work, eat, and sleep.

But he sought out opportunities to pray. He made prayer a priority, and he carved out time by himself—time to go away to "a place apart" and collect his thoughts and pray.

It wasn't easy for Jesus. It isn't easy for us, either.

And believe it or not, God gets that.

So ask him, "Got a minute?" Give him that much to begin with. Take that little moment of time and tell God what is on your mind. Make it direct. Make it clear. Make it plain.

It's that simple.

Leonard Bernstein's beautiful oratorio *Mass* starts with a wonderful musical meditation about the nature of God—and it offers some bold and surprising advice that all of us should take to heart. The oratorio begins with a tenor reminding himself—and the audience—that what he is undertaking (praying to God through the Mass) is less complicated than any of us may think.

"Sing God a simple song," he chants, "for God is the simplest of all."

> Mental prayer in my opinion is nothing else than an intimate sharing between friends. It means taking time frequently to be alone with Him who we know loves us. In order that love be true and the friendship endure, the wills of the friends must be in accord.
>
> —St. Teresa of Ávila[4]

> Sometimes I forget that God is present in the most mundane—even 'secular'—circumstances. I try to make that part of my daily prayer: seeking him in the ordinary moments of my day and raising the moment to God, even if just for an instant. It keeps me off balance, which is exactly where I need to be most of the time.
>
> —Dr. Barbara Golder, lawyer and editor,
> Chattanooga, Tennessee

We sometimes get frustrated when trying to pray because we think it has to be formal—following a particular template, or ritual, or formula. It doesn't. Remember the wisdom of St. Teresa: Prayer should be like a conversation with a friend. Talk to the Lord plainly, openly, honestly. He understands us better than we may think.

Be patient with yourself—because God most certainly is. What is on your mind? What is in your heart? If you had to sum up your prayer to God in a sentence, what would it be?

Dear God,

I stand before you with a million words to say,

a thousand thoughts to express,

but barely enough time, or energy, or skill to weave them together.

You know that already.

You know me already.

Help me.

Help me make sense of it all.

Help me find the words to express the inexpressible.

KEEPING IT SIMPLE

Help me to find peace in the midst of turmoil.
Help me to find calm in the midst of confusion.
Help me.
Even if I can't say what is in my heart, I know you will hear everything.
In you I place all my trust, all my confidence, all my hope.
You know my thoughts before I can speak them.
Take them for all they are;
accept them for all they may be,
in all their imperfection and awkwardness.
Accept everything, as I know you accept me,
and love me,
and want me to draw closer to you.
Thank you for making all things possible,
even this simple prayer.
Amen.

CHAPTER 4

HABIT FORMING

Rejoice in hope, endure in affliction, persevere in prayer.
—Romans 12:12

Shortly after I graduated from college, I moved into an apartment building a few blocks from a gym. I passed it every day while I was walking back and forth to work. After some months, at the start of a new year full of promise and too many calories from fruitcake and eggnog, I finally decided to take the plunge. I joined the gym.

I had the most committed, fulfilling, challenging, rewarding workouts of my life.

For about a month.

What started with zeal in January turned into tedium in February and became an evening on the couch eating cookies by March.

It can be the same when we talk about making a commitment to prayer.

We start out with high ideals and holy hearts, determined to pray.

Then comes the snooze alarm, and we want a few more minutes of sleep.

Or then comes the child with the school project.

Or the dog who needs to go to the vet.

Or the basement that floods.

Or the trip that takes you out of town for your job and leaves you with a headache, a sore neck, and the bitter aftertaste of too much coffee consumed on the long plane ride home.

Life gets in the way. And you think to yourself, "Dear God, when will it end?"

And look at that! You've just prayed!

Congratulations.

The fact is that if we want to become busy people who pray—instead of people who are always too busy to pray—we need to make prayer a priority. We need to *care* enough to carve out *time* enough to make this a part of our daily routine.

The easiest time to do this, of course, is at the beginning and end of the day—before the rush of deadlines and busyness crowds your mind—and then later, when you're getting ready to rest. Starting and ending the day with a word to God can make all the difference.

Years ago, a colleague at work gave me a beautiful wooden picture frame for Christmas, with a note: "My father always used to say, 'What matters in life is how you frame it.'" In this context, I have to think: *Doesn't it make sense for us to try to frame our days, our lives, in prayer?*

Greet the morning with a prayer of thanksgiving: "Thank you, Lord, for another day." Take five minutes to offer a prayer of praise and hope. Whisper the Lord's Prayer. Ask God for guidance. Thank him for whatever comes your way, and vow to accept all that unfolds as what it truly is: a gift.

Then, at the end of the day, try whispering it once again: "Thank you, Lord, for another day." Take time to take stock.

Consider where the day led you, where *God* led you. Ask God for the grace to continue to grow and learn—and the desire to draw closer to him. (More on this later, by the way.)

In time, you may start to see your prayer life, like so many other aspects of life, develop a rhythm all its own. Your days gain a blessed structure—a frame—that helps hold everything together.

You are developing the important practice of making prayer a *habit*—something that slides naturally into the ebb and flow of your life. Some find that it helps to carve out a corner of the home as a "prayer corner," a kind of sacred space that may have little more than a chair, a table, a cross, and a lamp for reading. They make this place a daily destination where nothing else matters but the most important conversation, that ongoing dialogue with God.

Wherever you pray, whenever you pray, commit to it. Start with five minutes every day. Then ten. You may find the habit of prayer growing on you.

Your prayer doesn't have to be perfect. It doesn't have to be complete. It just has to *be*. All you really need is the desire to speak to God in whatever way is easiest—and trust him to make it even easier.

Every Moment Is Grace

Personally, I've found one of the most convenient places to pray isn't even above ground. It's on the subway, on the way to work.

Let's face it: in the early hours of a weekday morning, heading to work, we are all transients. For a few minutes, we are cohabitants, neighbors, bound by time and space and dirty plastic seats, blinking at one another as the lights flicker, the windows rattle, and the stops go hurtling by in a blizzard of white tile.

I'm taking the train earlier these days; I usually step onto the subway platform in Queens around 7:30 a.m., to get to work around 8:15 a.m. I often take the local; it's easier to get a seat. But sometimes I'll take the express and stand, spending a few moments struggling to stay awake. (Here's a quick prayer for you: "Dear God, keep me from falling asleep and missing my stop . . .") It's interesting to see what people are doing at that hour.

A lot of people do Sudoku puzzles these days, from a paperback book or the newspaper. A few still struggle with the crossword. Some take the *New York Times* and fold it into long rectangles for easy reading (it's a peculiar New York form of origami, I think). Some read paperbacks by Grisham or King or Steele. Once in a while, a young man with a yarmulke, dressed in black, will step into the train and crack open a book in Hebrew. Sometimes I'll see older ladies with little pamphlets, reading lessons from the Bible.

YOUR PRAYER DOESN'T HAVE TO BE PERFECT. IT DOESN'T HAVE TO BE COMPLETE. IT JUST HAS TO *BE*.

One morning I caught sight of a very serious young woman seated across from me, hands folded, eyes closed, lips moving. And as I looked down at her hands, I noticed they were fingering beads. She was praying the Rosary.

I've seen that before. Like that folded *New York Times*, it's a New York phenomenon, a prayerful habit that suggests that we are a distinctly devout city, full of immigrants and varied cultures that are constantly rubbing up against each other and giving people a lot of reasons to pray. But that particular morning, I found it unexpectedly moving. This young woman was in prayer—a special, profoundly personal, kind of prayer.

"Pray for us sinners, now and at the hour of our death. Amen."

In a hole in the ground, rattling under a river, surrounded by darkness and strangers, one of the anonymous throng herded into a tin box was praying to a woman full of grace.

Subways are a mystery. They shouldn't work, but they do, and it's a minor miracle we aren't swallowed alive by the earth. But that morning, one of my neighbors on the subway—a traveler on this journey, a fellow transient, a pilgrim bound for points unknown—was embracing another mystery. She was holding it in her hands.

As I thought about that and looked around the subway car, I understood that we had become a kind of church, each of us deep into our own silent prayers of Sudoku or stock market news or sports scores or gossip columns.

Or deep into prayers to Mary.

If you commute every day as I do, take those few moments between here and there, between where you are and where you're headed, to offer a prayer of expectation, of gratitude, of hope. Life, after all, is a journey. Shouldn't we make it one of prayer?

Find comfort in knowing you are not alone. None of us are. Understanding that, and embracing that, is a kind of prayer itself.

That morning on the train, I looked again at the woman with the rosary and saw her smile to herself. And I smiled too.

A subway car of strangers was no longer merely full of people.

To those who choose to believe, it was full of grace.

This is how it can be in our daily lives as well. Try it. You may be astonished at what happens.

> If you really wish to follow Christ, if you want your love for him to grow and last, then you must be *faithful to prayer*. It is *the key to the vitality of your life in Christ*. Without prayer, your faith and love will die. If you are constant in daily prayer and in the Sunday celebration of Mass, your love for Jesus will increase. And your heart will know deep joy and peace, such as the world could never give.
>
> —Pope St. John Paul II[5]

Try praying every day for a sustained period. Thirty minutes is a good goal, but start with ten minutes. There are different ways to pray, such as saying the Rosary or reading from the Bible, so make a plan and stick to it. Try to find a focal point and pray away from distractions: turn off your cell phone and leave it in a separate room, for example, or set up a prayer corner.

> And try to change up your prayer a little bit. Every Christian is asked to pray daily, but there is no rule about what to pray, and there are many different and good ways to pray.
> — Fr. Matthew Schneider, LC, Washington, DC

One tip for successfully integrating prayer into our daily lives is to make it a habit, so try to make daily prayer part of your routine. Carve out a few minutes, the same few minutes, every day. First thing in the morning? Perfect. Before you brew the coffee, check in with God. Riding to work with nothing to do? Have a few words with the Lord. Share with him your concerns about the day ahead. Ask him to stay close. Find a few minutes and make that your "God time." Then stick to it.

After a while, you'll be surprised at how natural it becomes—and you'll be grateful for the small but meaningful ways the habit of prayer can help refocus your life. Be attentive. Be disciplined. But also be patient and merciful with yourself. Habits aren't formed overnight. Years ago, I heard the singer Harry Connick admit, "I'm a practicing Catholic. I'm going to keep practicing until I get it right." Keep practicing prayer!

Dear God,
Here I am again,
trying to make time to pray.
You know it isn't easy for me.
But you know, too, how much I want this,
and how much I believe you want to help me.
Can you give me a hand?
In my trying, please see my effort,
my intention,
my hope,
and my love for you.
In my struggles, please see my yearning,
my desire,
my searching,
and my love for you.
You can give shape to my days
and order to my life.
Your tenderness and support
make the impossible possible.
So, dear God,
help frame my life in prayer.
Give that frame four sides:

faith,

hope,

love,

and courage.

The courage to persist.

The courage to trust in you.

Now and always.

Amen.

CHAPTER 5

"PRAY WITHOUT CEASING"? ARE YOU KIDDING ME?

Rejoice always. Pray without ceasing. In all circumstances give thanks, for this is the will of God for you in Christ Jesus.

—1 Thessalonians 5:16-18

When I was a teenager, I spent one summer washing dishes and busing tables at Gifford's Ice Cream Parlor in Silver Spring, Maryland. I can still remember the relentless smell of melting ice cream mingling with the soapy scent of dishwashing detergent.

It was pretty disgusting.

Honestly, I couldn't eat ice cream all that summer. The thought of it made me queasy. I spent my afternoons and evenings up to my elbows in half-eaten chocolate sundaes with melted cream, deflated cherries, and soggy sprinkles. Thankfully, in time I recovered. Ice cream isn't a problem anymore (though my doctor and my wife might disagree).

Anyway, I had reason to remember that summer when I picked up a copy of *The Practice of the Presence of God* by an obscure Carmelite named Nicolas Herman, better known as Brother Lawrence.

Centuries ago, Brother Lawrence crafted a simple but profound form of spirituality that has captivated generations of believers. I think it offers us a model for making prayer not only one part of our lives, but really the greatest part. Practicing the presence of God transforms the very act of living into an enduring, ongoing prayer—a way to pray without ceasing.

Nicolas Herman was born in France in 1614. He was wounded in military service and while recovering, he decided he wanted to become a monk. When he was twenty-six, he entered the Order of Discalced Carmelites in Paris as a lay brother and took the religious name of Lawrence.

It was not what anyone might consider glamorous. He worked in the monastery kitchen, cooking meals for the friars. In later years, he turned to sandal making. That was about as exciting as his life got.

It was busy, it was tedious, it was . . . uninspiring.

Brother Lawrence found the life of a monk not nearly as uplifting as he expected. He prayed, he meditated, he spent hours in silence. And none of it really fulfilled him. Instead, he developed his own unique form of spirituality by training himself to practice being in God's presence.

And it happened just by doing the dishes. As he wrote,

WANT TO "PRAY WITHOUT CEASING"? BEGIN BY MAKING EVERY ACT, EVERY GESTURE, EVERY TASK A FORM OF PRAYER. GIVE IT TO GOD.

> I gave up all devotions and prayers that were not required and I devote myself exclusively to remaining always in his holy presence. I keep myself in his presence by simple attentiveness and a

> general loving awareness of God that I call "actual presence of God" or better, a quiet and secret conversation of the soul with God that is lasting.[6]

Brother Lawrence died in obscurity at the age of seventy-seven, and the slender book he left behind is a small but beautiful treasure. It amounts to his own sort of "rule," a guide for all who want to turn everyday living into an ongoing prayer.

Of life in the kitchen, he wrote,

> The times of activity are not at all different from the hours of prayer, for I possess God as peacefully in the commotion of my kitchen, where often people are asking me for different things at the same time, as I do when kneeling in front of the Blessed Sacrament.[7]

Pots and Pans and Prayer

To this day, Brother Lawrence remains a vital witness to something many of us neglect or overlook: prayer is infinitely creative and adaptable. It can—and should!—involve all of what we are. We pray to the Lord as his creation, as incarnate beings who toil, struggle, rejoice, and, yes, work. Want to "pray without ceasing"? Begin by making every act, every gesture, every task a form of prayer. Give it to God. Offer it at the sink, in the garage, on the bus, in the garden, in the cubicle behind a pile of papers waiting to be filed.

Any work, offered with love to the Lord, can be a prayer if we intend it to be. Really.

Answering the phone, tending the garden, typing a term paper, balancing a checkbook, changing a diaper, bandaging a wound—all this and more are part of God's infinitely wondrous and imperfect world.

We can do more than just perform these tasks. We can *pray* them.

When I was growing up, my mother had a small prayer plaque hanging over the sink in our kitchen. I see the same prayer for sale in gift shops today and hanging in church rectories. "The Kitchen Prayer" speaks to the devotion of Brother Lawrence and the everyday piety that so many of us strive to live.

Klara Munkres, a retired schoolteacher from Savannah, Missouri, wrote the prayer. She died in 1971, and though most people have never heard of her, countless people know her words.

This plainly stated but heartfelt little poem has gone on to become one of the most widely read devotions of its kind in the world—an ode to prayerful domesticity and a petition to help us find God and his presence everywhere:

Lord of all pots and pans and things
Since I've not time to be
A saint by doing lovely things or
Watching late with Thee
Or dreaming in the dawn light or

Storming Heaven's gates
Make me a saint by getting meals and
Washing up the plates.

Although I must have Martha's hands,
I have a Mary mind
And when I black the boots and shoes,
Thy sandals Lord I find.
I think of how they trod the earth,
What time I scrub the floor
Accept this meditation Lord,
I haven't time for more.

Warm all the kitchen with Thy love,
And light it with Thy peace
Forgive me all my worrying and make
My grumbling cease.
Thou who didst love to give men food,
In room or by the sea
Accept this service that I do,
I do it unto Thee.

Klara Munkres was on to something—capturing the serenity that can come from doing anything and *everything* for God.

Brother Lawrence, five centuries earlier, understood that to pray without ceasing was not as difficult as it may sound. He mastered the theology of presence, the gift of being present to God, and turned that deep awareness into a minute-by-minute practice. His secret? "I apply myself diligently to do nothing and think nothing which may displease him. I hope that when I have done what I can, he will do with me what he pleases."[8]

It sounds simple enough, but the challenge is huge. It is the work of a lifetime—which, when I was a teenager, was the way I felt about washing dishes at an ice cream parlor.

But the benefits of the kind of lifelong prayer described by Brother Lawrence last longer.

And the scent is infinitely sweeter.

> It is not necessary for being with God to be always at church; we may make an oratory of our heart, wherein to retire from time to time, to converse with him in meekness, humility, and love. Every one is capable of such familiar conversation with God, some more, some less.
>
> —Brother Lawrence[9]

> I think we have to open up the definition of prayer to be more inclusive, more active. Sculpting is prayer; in my studio, prayer is action; it is on the move. To our disadvantage, prayer has become something still and distilled as if—you move, you break the spell. If I create a sculpture of Jesus, I feel I am praying in an aggressive way, inventing, doing. I think this type of prayer is open to life's interruptions,

maybe perceived by some as a mild type of prayer, but over time perhaps more potent than one hour of silent prayer in a church.

Perhaps we have made the idea of prayer too sacred so that no one does it anymore, like the good silverware that is only set out for special occasions.

For more than three years, as I work—usually for eight hours at a time, every day—I listen to unabridged Bible recordings on repeat. Previous generations have not had this opportunity. I go in and out of the text through my work. I take a phone call, get a tool, but the Bible is always there to settle back into. It is the audio landscape of my studio. Again, it might seem like a mild form of prayer, but sometimes it awakens moments that are very spiritual. This is part of my prayer.

—Timothy Schmalz, sculptor of Homeless Jesus, Ontario, Canada

Too often, we think of prayer as something we start, then finish, then get back to at some other time. It's words and actions. Sometimes, we pray by rote. We formalize prayer and ritualize it. We speak it, sing it, chant it, recite it. That's good, and it is beautiful, and it can serve to orient our hearts.

But there is another way.

Just for today, consider your life, every moment of it, to be a prayer.

Consider your chores to be a prayer.

Consider your commute, your breakfast, your lunch, your meetings, your time spent on the phone on hold, all to be a prayer. Even your time on Facebook or answering emails can be, should be, transformed into a prayer.

Give it to God. Do it for him. Do it *with* him. Every hour can be an hour prayed without ceasing.

Your conversations with your family are a prayer. Time spent with your spouse is a prayer. God has made you for these moments and for so many more.

Make of your day a prayer. Just for one day.

In time, with a little practice, your very existence—every breath, smile, laugh, sigh—will become a living psalm.

Dear God,
Just for today, I give you everything.
I give you my waking and my sleeping,
my hunger and my satisfaction.
I give you my frustration and my joy,
my stress and my boredom.
I give you everything.
With all my imperfections and all my weaknesses,
I give you all that I am.
And I do it all with love,
because I know your love brought me into being.
You loved me enough to give me this life,
and I want to live it for you.
I give you everything I create
and everything I toss aside.
I give you the memo I hated writing
and the meeting I hated attending.
I give you the stale toast I had for breakfast
and the limp salad I had for lunch.
And I give you the slice of cheesecake I had for desert,
even though I'm trying to lose weight . . .
I give you everything.
This is my life. This is my prayer.

I offer you my sadness, my loneliness, my tiredness, and my tedium.
But I offer you my excitement, my enthusiasm, my friendships, and my joy.
You are my God. I am your handiwork.
And this is my prayer:
Every moment, all for you.
Take my life as it is; take me as I am.
And take it all with my thanksgiving and my love.
It's all I can give, and I give it to you.
This is my life. This is my prayer.
Thank you for making it so.
Amen.

CHAPTER 6

AMAZING GRACE: PRAYING BEFORE MEALS

Let them thank the LORD for his mercy, such wondrous deeds for the children of Adam. For he satisfied the thirsty, filled the hungry with good things.
—Psalm 107:8-9

Got ten seconds? Then you have time to say one of the most familiar prayers in the world: grace before meals. Seriously. I clocked it. You can do this in about ten seconds—and even that humble act can serve to connect you, however briefly, with the Creator of all you are about to receive.

At every meal, my wife and I take a moment to quietly pray together words that most of us learned before we were out of our childhood high chairs:

Bless us, O Lord,
and these, thy gifts,
which we are about to receive
through thy bounty,
through Christ, our Lord,
Amen.

It's one of the most familiar prayers we Catholics utter—right up there with the Our Father and Hail Mary. And I suspect most of us don't give it more than a passing thought. (Did someone say "passing"? Pass the potatoes! Let's eat!) But if you are looking for a way to add prayer to your busy life, I'd like to make a suggestion: make those words the first course of every meal.

Before you slice the ham, carve the turkey, ladle the soup, or sprinkle the salt, take a moment to serve up a helping of grace.

I know, it's fallen out of fashion. You rarely see people doing this at a restaurant or at dinner anymore. But try making the saying of grace part of your mealtime ritual. Trust and believe that there is grace in this.

Amazing grace.

It is the grace that comes from stopping everything you are doing for yourself in order to do something for the Lord: thank him. As you ask him to bless what you are about to eat, consider where this food came from—*who* it came from—and think for a moment about all that went into the steaming gravy, succulent meat, and buttery vegetables.

I'd also suggest thinking—*really thinking*—about what you are saying. Listen to those words as they escape your lips.

"Bless us, O Lord . . ." Father, confer on us your blessing, a generous act of love that we really do not deserve. (Except the pie, of course. Everyone deserves pie.)

"And these, thy gifts . . ." While you're at it, could you also bless the food sitting before us? (Especially the pie . . . but if broccoli is involved, okay, you can bless that too.) Seeing this food on our table when we know others are going hungry, we realize that this is all part of a harvest you have graciously provided. It is truly a gift.

"Which we are about to receive . . ." The gift has been given, and we are about to accept it into our hearts, and into our bodies. (That sound you hear, Lord, is our stomachs rumbling. Don't be alarmed. But dinner smells so good.)

"Through thy bounty . . ." But we cannot forget that this meal is here because of your ever-generous creation, your bounty. The food before us is the fruit of the earth you made, the soil you enriched, the seeds you allowed to bud from ripening plants, the creatures you placed on this earth to roam the fields, feed at the rivers, and nest in the trees. It's all yours. And it is also, in some way, ours (especially the pie).

"Through Christ, our Lord . . ." We ask all this through your beloved Son, our savior and brother, Jesus Christ. (If he were here, we'd be happy to share the pie with him.)

"*Amen.*" To all that we have asked, and all that we have offered, we can add only one word: *Amen*. The punctuation at the end of every prayer, the affirmation at the end of every hope. *Yes.* We seal this with our hearts, and with our assent (and maybe with whipped cream).

Want to vary your prayer life? Other religious traditions have beautiful prayers before meals that share similar sentiments:

- Come, Lord Jesus, be our Guest, and let these gifts to us be blessed. Amen. (Lutheran)
- Be present at our table, Lord. Be here and everywhere adored. These mercies bless and grant that we may feast in fellowship with thee. Amen. (Methodist)

- O Christ our God, bless the food and drink of your servants, for you are holy, always, now and ever, and forever. Amen. (Byzantine Catholic)

Don't Just Say It; Pray It

Some families like to improvise the prayer before a meal, or even make an exercise out of it, asking different children to offer the prayer each night. The important thing isn't who prays, but the sentiment behind it—that those present at the table lift up their hearts in gratitude and charity.

Saying grace is the most effortless prayer we can offer. And we usually forget it before the first forkful leaves the table. But every now and then, it is good to take a moment, take a deep breath, and make every word matter. (It doesn't hurt, of course, to practice this prayerful self-awareness and thoughtfulness with all forms of prayer that can easily become, by repetition, rote and routine.)

Our lives and our meals are enriched when we don't just *say* grace but *pray* it.

OUR LIVES AND OUR MEALS ARE ENRICHED WHEN WE DON'T JUST SAY GRACE, BUT *PRAY* IT.

In summary: Pray, first and foremost, with gratitude—the gratitude we usually only muster at Thanksgiving, with the nice china, and the clean linens, and the distant cousins who drove in from Pittsburgh.

Gratitude is itself a kind of prayer, a prayer of thanksgiving (with a small "t"). And what better place to pray in thanksgiving than when gathered around the table?

The German mystic and philosopher Meister Eckhart once wrote, "If the only prayer you ever said in your whole life was 'thank you,' that would suffice."[10]

Say "thank you" to God—and not only for the food.

Our gratitude doesn't end when the prayer stops and we pass around the bread basket. Every beat of your heart affirms an unmistakable mystery: God has given you life. Extravagant, beautiful, painful, challenging *life*.

What a wonder that is!

Let's embrace God's blessings wherever we find them, however they come to us. And let's give thanks for them, every day, in every moment.

Pray not only for what *we* have, but pray also for those who *don't* have. Pray for those who prepared the food—everyone from the farmers who grew it, to the store clerks who stocked it, to the parent who zapped it in the microwave.

So try grace before meals. No life can ever be too busy to give, even briefly, a word of thanks to almighty God for something as simple and satisfying as a warm meal and a full stomach—especially in our troubled world where so many are going without.

Take a moment to think about what all these blessings mean.

Take a moment to reflect, remember, and pray.

You just might find yourself going back for seconds.

Our prayer opens the door to God who teaches us to come out of ourselves constantly, to make us capable of being close to others to bring them comfort, hope and light, especially at moments of trial. May the Lord grant us to be capable of increasingly more intense prayer, in order to strengthen our personal relationship with God the Father, to open our heart to the needs of those beside us.

—Pope Benedict XVI[11]

The quantity of prayer is not always its truest measure. What matters most is the quality of even a few prayers, prayed with an awareness of God's presence, with both understanding and feeling, and with the mind and the heart. . . . Prayer before holy icons trains the inner eye of the soul to recognize the sacred image of God in ourselves and our neighbor.

If we wish to come into the sacramental presence of Christ in our homes, open the Gospels before an icon of Christ and speak his holy name in prayer.

—Deacon Daniel Dozier, St. George the Great Martyr Byzantine Catholic Church, Olympia, Washington

If you find yourself struggling to make time for prayer and make a habit of it, here's a good way to start: grace. Make a point of saying grace before every meal, wherever you are—at the kitchen table, at McDonald's, at a fancy French restaurant celebrating a special occasion, anywhere. Take a moment; close your eyes. At a fast-food restaurant? Picture others who have sat at that same plastic table, picking up a burger or fries. Whisper a prayer for those anonymous strangers, whoever they are, wherever they might be. At a diner? A cafeteria? Thank God for that!

Remember this: Jesus's first miracle took place with wine; later he multiplied loaves and fishes, and he capped his earthly life with the greatest meal of all the night before he died. God clearly saw beauty and something sacred in what people do when gathered around a table. So should we.

Dear God,
You feed me and those I love.
Thank you.
Give me the grace to always thank you.
And help me to remember at this moment others who are hungry.
Those who hunger for food,
but also those who hunger for other things,
like love or friendship or security or dignity.
May your grace help me to remember
those I can so easily forget.
Bless all that I receive
and all those whose work puts food on the table—
the farmers, the cooks, and the servers.
May all of us treasure the bounty you bring us,
including the greatest bounty of all:
your grace.
Your amazing grace.
Amen.

CHAPTER 7

CAN YOU HEAR ME NOW? THE POWER OF SILENCE

"Speak, for your servant is listening."
—1 Samuel 3:10

Too often, we think of prayer as a monologue—a torrent of words we have to speak, recite, chant, or read. We expect God to sit there, politely listening, nodding, and carefully taking notes.

Poor, patient God—he can't get a word in edgewise.

Which brings me to a critically important part of prayer: listening! In prayer, we need to *listen* to what God has to say to us and give him time and space to speak to us.

We need to offer him, and ourselves, the bliss of blessed silence. An old adage tells us that silence is golden. In prayer, I'd give it an upgrade. Silence is platinum.

Modern life, of course, doesn't help.

As previously noted, I live and work in New York City. The soundtrack of daily life includes horns, trucks, train whistles, jets, boom boxes, car alarms, and jackhammers. At any given moment, the building where I live reverberates with the stereophonic sound of a baby crying, a couple arguing, a door slamming, a dog yapping, or the guy downstairs warming up on his trumpet before heading out to play a recital. (He also has a massive sound system hooked up to his TV. Saturday nights often include the floor vibrating from the attack on Pearl Harbor, or an asteroid striking the earth, or Jedi marching through a galaxy far, far away.)

So how do you find some silence in the middle of the noise in your life? It takes effort.

Trick #1: noise-canceling headphones. A little music piped in from my iPhone, and I'm transported to another time and place.

Trick #2: the bathroom. Yes, the bathroom. Go in, shut the door, and the world melts away.

Trick #3: climb under the covers, wrap the pillow around your head, and hide. It works. Really.

But the most important trick, really, is to trick yourself. Seek silence wherever you can, however you can. Be still. Be silent. Close your ears. Close your eyes. Then open your mind and heart to what God is trying to tell you.

Cardinal Robert Sarah has written extensively on this subject and even devoted an entire book to it, *The Power of Silence*. The book's to-the-point subtitle is *Against the Dictatorship of Noise*. He put it beautifully:

> It is necessary to leave our interior turmoil in order to find God. Despite the agitations, the busyness, the easy pleasures, God remains silently present. He is in us like a thought, a word, and

> a presence whose secret sources are buried in God himself, inaccessible to human inspection. Solitude is the best state in which to hear God's silence.[12]

The Art of Silence

Monks and mystics are adept at this sort of thing, and you'll find a lot of sage advice on how to pray in silence from writers like Basil Pennington, Thomas Keating, and Thomas Merton. These Trappist monks mastered the art of prayer in empty chapels, in near-darkness, in the middle of nowhere, in the middle of the night.

That was how I first discovered the power of silence, and listening, and their importance to prayer.

"In a real dark night of the soul," wrote F. Scott Fitzgerald, "it is always three o'clock in the morning."[13] Fitzgerald should have waited another hour. The dawn begins to break at four.

That's when the monks pray Vigils at the Monastery of the Holy Spirit in Conyers, Georgia. And it was there, at four in the morning, that I saw the sun begin to rise even though outside it remained pitch-black.

I was in Conyers for a private retreat—three days at the Trappist monastery in a spare room with a bed, a desk, a chair, and a lamp. And books. I brought lots of books.

Settling in on Friday evening, I leafed through the literature in my room, including the schedule for liturgies and a pamphlet with testimonials from others who had been there before me.

I had planned to skip Vigils and get up in time for Lauds at seven—much more reasonable, I thought. Who needs to pray in the middle of the night?

Well, leafing through those testimonials made me feel like *I* did. Time and again, the former guests sang the praises of the night Vigils. To miss that, they implied, would be like going to China and skipping the Great Wall. Reluctantly I agreed to give this Vigil stuff a shot. I set my alarm for 3:45 a.m. and turned out the light.

A few moments later, I was shaken by a sound that burned my disbelieving ears: my alarm.

3:45? Already?

I could hear the thump-thump of footfalls up and down the hall—other guests scurrying to church. I weighed skipping out, taking a pass. Wouldn't a couple more hours of slumber do me good? I waited for the answer. It didn't come. So I got up.

I threw on a t-shirt, staggered into the bathroom, splashed the sleep from my eyes, blinked into the fluorescent light, and made my way downstairs to the church.

I slipped in through the side door. Other, hardier souls were already up and poised for prayer. Monks in their choir, guests in their pews. I padded to the rear of the church, sat on a squeaky bench, and gazed at a quiet world stirring awake.

"Unbelievable" is the one-word description Flannery O'Connor used to describe this very church, decades ago, when it was new. She was right. It defies mere belief.

This soaring abbey church is a prayer—a psalm in stone, grace in stained glass. Its arches bend above, like hands meeting in meditation, fingertips touching. It contains within it everything needed to attune the soul and focus the eyes. It soothes and celebrates, all in one breath.

I barely had time to absorb this before the monks began their chant—a low murmur of praise and thanksgiving. Lights burned on the walls, and candles glowed by the tabernacle behind the altar. Among the monks, there was bowing, shuffling, the flutter of pages being turned. For twenty minutes or so, they sang, prayed, and whispered. And then they were done.

Silently, they slipped from the choir. One by one, the lights of the church dimmed. In an instant, the monks had vanished, becoming shadows, joining the darkening corners of the nave.

And there we sat, guests of the abbey, in our spindly wooden pews—and guests, also, at a mystery that was just beginning to unfold.

One's eyes couldn't help but be drawn to the tabernacle and the altar where candles continued to glow, providing the only light in the church.

It was late July, yet the air was uncommonly cool. The doors of the church were open to the Georgia fields, and a small breeze crept in, through, and around the church. I could hear leaves moving, crickets singing—nature unfolding its own psalm book, fingering the ribbon and finding the page to begin another day.

And so much silence. Exquisite silence.

In this prayer of a church, on this canticle of a morning, silence said everything I needed to hear. And with nothing to hear, really, but the beating of my own heart and the gentle rustling of the world outside, it was infinitely easier for me to find the words to talk to God.

And talk we did.

We spoke of thanksgiving and gratitude, of generosity and of greed. We talked of friends, family, work. We confided thoughts of love and loss; we examined worry, woe, and unsettled grievances. And when thoughts of the world and all its perils overwhelmed my bewildered heart, God and I simply savored the silence and agreed that sometimes there is nothing that needs to be said. He understood. That was all I needed to know.

And so it was that there in that church, seated on a plain wooden plank in the darkest hour of the morning, I saw the dawn begin to break. The world was still blackness and shadow and the flickering of candles.

But in my heart, it was sunrise.

The silence had done its job. It made it easier for me to speak to God. And for him, in fact, to speak to me. I slipped out of my pew and back to my room—astonished and at peace, and blissfully, cheerfully awake.

AN OLD ADAGE TELLS US THAT SILENCE IS GOLDEN. IN PRAYER, I'D GIVE IT AN UPGRADE. SILENCE IS PLATINUM.

The early monastics who established these fixed hours of prayer knew, it seems, something about the importance of Vigil prayer. Here, after the dark night of the soul, the day awaits. We begin again.

I finally understood what all the previous guests at the retreat house were talking about. I'd made it to China and had seen the Great Wall.

And it is, indeed, a wonder.

Of course, not everyone can make a retreat to a distant monastery, in the middle of a cornfield, on a summer night. But you don't need to. Turn off the TV. Shut off the computer. Dim the lights. And ask God, in the middle of whatever silence you can find, wherever you can find it, to tell you what's on his mind.

It can be the start of a great conversation.

> When I am liberated by silence, when I am no longer involved in the measurement of life, but in the living of it, I can discover a form of prayer in which there is effectively no distraction. My whole life becomes a prayer. My whole silence is full of prayer. The world of silence in which I am immersed contributes to my prayer.
>
> —Thomas Merton[14]

I am a very distracted person. I come from a retail background in my earlier life, and stopping to quiet myself for prayer has always been a challenge! One thing that has helped me over the years is to take advantage of times that I'm my own captive audience. One of the best of those times is when I'm in the car. I'm the sort of a person who gets in the car and puts on the radio for news, or tunes into an FM station for music. I have disciplined myself to simply get in the car and not do any of that.

The silence of the car is the place I can be most quiet, especially on a longer drive. I'm not calling God my excuse for distracted driving, but I have been able to talk to God in that space where neither he nor I can get away. Okay, so it's not very meditational prayer. I can't close my eyes—you don't want to be coming the other way in another car if that happens! But I can communicate with the Lord about what is happening that day, where I need his help big-time, and then hear that wonderful small voice that assures all of us that he is with us. It's not the only way I pray, but some days it's the best way to keep the Lord in mind as I go about my day.

—Fr. Daniel Pacholec, Springfield, Massachusetts

Seek out silence.

The hum of daily life is always tempting us with the sort of "sound and fury" that signify nothing, to paraphrase Shakespeare's Macbeth. You don't have to let the noise of life grind you down. Look for ways to lower the volume, find a quiet space, and offer a moment or two to God. If you can, go to a church that is open during the day. The flicker of candles and the hush of the sacred can adjust your thinking and direct your thoughts.

And wherever your thoughts may go, God will be there, waiting to hear them and ready to give you some feedback.

So, be silent. Be patient. Be still.

Open your heart. And trust God to do the rest.

Dear God,
So often I'm the one doing all the talking.
Pleading, praising, pondering.
So often during prayer, the noise of life gets in the way.
Just for this moment,
just for now,
help me to hear what you have to say.
Guide me to listen to you,
even when it seems that silence is your only language.
Open my heart.
Touch my soul.
Be with me in my searching.
Walk with me on my journey.
Help to listen to you more closely,
as I know you listen to me.
Speak, Lord, and tell me what is on your mind.
Amen.

CHAPTER 8

THE RITE STUFF: LITURGY AS PRAYER

Them I will bring to my holy mountain and make them joyful in my house of prayer; their burnt offerings and their sacrifices will be acceptable on my altar, for my house shall be called a house of prayer for all peoples.
—Isaiah 56:7

A folding chair on a linoleum floor—that's my earliest memory of church. The space was large, with a high ceiling, bad lighting, and giant fans in the corners that blew around the deadly hot summer air. This was St. Peter's Catholic Church in Olney, Maryland, and I was, at most, four years old when I began to notice some of these details. The place where the parish worshipped was a big hall that included a plain altar set on a stage for Mass. We unfolded a cheap, plastic dividing wall, like a big accordion, to hide the altar when we didn't need it. The church was, in fact, a multipurpose room, used also as the school auditorium, the cafeteria, and theater.

We did everything in that space, including going to Mass.

There was no crying room. There were no special liturgies for children. But families poured into this space anyway—some of them with six or seven kids. I remember, vaguely, the Mass being said in Latin, before the reforms of Vatican

Council II. Not attending Mass on any given Sunday would have been, God forbid, unthinkable.

Over the years, my church-going and Mass-going have included anything and everything: soaring cathedrals, cramped conference rooms, hotel ballrooms, cruise ship dining rooms, and even a time or two, a hotel guest room where we used the desk as an altar. Catholic liturgy, I have discovered, is remarkably flexible. God is everywhere, after all—and he is able to accommodate a surprisingly wide array of circumstances and spaces.

In all of these settings, often to my amazement and awe, I've been blessed to be able to pray what Pope Benedict XVI called "the greatest and highest prayer," the Mass.

Lest we forget: when we take time to attend Mass, we are taking time to pray on an epic scale. Mass is the all-consuming prayer par excellence. You get to receive the Eucharist, Jesus Christ himself, in the form of bread and wine, and you get to raise your voice in prayer through responses, praise, petitions, thanksgiving, and (very often) song. Looking for the ultimate way to pray? You can't beat the Mass.

LOOKING FOR THE ULTIMATE WAY TO PRAY? YOU CAN'T BEAT THE MASS.

All of this means that, for a busy person trying to find time to pray, one of the best and most efficient ways is one you may not have considered: going to Mass!

That hour at the beginning of the week can do more to lift the heart, stir the soul, and engage the mind than you may realize. Caveat: yes, I know that not all Masses are memorable. Since they require human engagement and involvement, they suffer from very human problems. Sometimes the preaching is weak, the music is lame, the atmosphere is dull, and the people around you are glaring at your children or rolling their eyes at your Sunday attire. Sleeping in can seem like a much holier (and pleasurable) use of your time.

But attending Mass is one of the great privileges and treasures of our faith—and, really, of our country too. I work for an agency of the Holy See that ministers to some of the poorest and most desperate corners of the world. People in parts of India, Ethiopia, and Syria are starving for the Eucharist and would do almost anything to be in a country where they could attend Mass every week—let alone every day!—no matter how lackluster the experience might seem. These people don't mind having to worship in a leaky tent before a makeshift card table altar; they don't grumble (as we so often do) about inconvenient Mass times or a crowded parking lot. It's Mass! It's Jesus in the Eucharist! It's a miracle unfolding in human hands, placing Christ before us and bringing him into us.

Don't we get that?

We should. We must.

We Pray as One

If you want to carve out just one hour for prayer during a frenzied, busy week, make it that hour during Mass. Your life will be immeasurably enriched.

If you have more time, take a few minutes to familiarize yourself with the readings before you go. Pray over them. Pull out your Bible, and read what comes before and what comes after those passages that make up the readings for the day. Dip into the context, the history, the background. Want to be even better prepared? Look over the opening and concluding prayers for the Mass. Take a few minutes before you leave the house to quietly reflect on what you are about to experience.

Then let go—and let God.

There is also something to be said—a lot, actually—about the simple act of "corporate" prayer. Part of what makes the experience of Mass so distinct is that we do it together as the body of Christ, as a people gathered in one place for one express purpose: to worship our God and to receive the grace of the Eucharist.

Our participation in Mass helps to underscore a beautiful, fundamental fact of our faith: Christianity is not a solitary act. We live it most fully and practice it most completely when we are with others. We join our hearts and prayers to a wider communion—the communion of saints and the communion of the faithful around the world. We continue what was begun at the Last Supper, what was celebrated in secret in the catacombs, what has been prayed, and believed, and carried forth by innumerable generations, in many languages, in tiny chapels and soaring cathedrals, in every corner of the globe for two millennia.

We pray as one.

And the source and summit of it all is something that appears to be nothing more than a sliver of bread—as weightless as paper, no bigger than a coin.

Behold, the Lamb of God.

Pope St. John Paul II summed it up simply: "The Eucharist is the secret of my day," he once said. "It gives strength and meaning to all my activities of service to the Church and to the whole world."[15]

No matter how busy we are, how preoccupied we feel, how distracted and overwhelmed we become, this is where the rubber meets the road.

Want to pray? Want to make prayer more central to your life? Mark off an hour every week to go to Mass.

You can thank me later.

> God wants to save us in a people. He does not want to save us in isolation. . . . The church wants to rouse men and women to the true meaning of being a people. . . . What is a people? A people is a community of persons where all cooperate for the common good.
>
> —St. Oscar Romero[16]

> God is present in everything. In the universe, in creation, in me and all that happens to me, in my brothers and sisters, in the church—everywhere.
>
> —Sr. Thea Bowman, FSPA[17]

The Church has called us to "fully conscious and active participation" in the Mass, which is the most perfect form of prayer (Constitution on the Sacred Liturgy, 14). How can we do that better? Try taking time before Mass to look over the readings—maybe even read some of the passages that come immediately before and after the readings in order to get a sense of context. Is there a recurring theme? What is God trying to say to me in these readings this week? During Mass, listen closely to the individual prayers. Make the effort to pray, really pray, some of the words that have become so familiar to you over the years, from the Lord's Prayer to the Gloria or the Creed.

This is the collective voice of the Church! Remind yourself that you are not praying alone. You are praying in communion and in community—not just with those around you, but with countless unseen believers around the world and with the saints in heaven. For this one hour of the week, give yourself totally to simply being in the presence of God. Where will he guide you? Where will you go in the days to come? Trust that he will be by your side.

Dear God,
Here I am.
It is another Sunday morning at Mass.
Thank you for the gift of this day
and the opportunity to be with you in your house.
In the hour to come, help to remember:
no sin is too great,
no problem is too large,
no burden is too heavy
that you cannot help me.
This day, I make of my life an offering to you.
I praise you for the world you have made.
I thank you for the life you have given me.
I open my arms to welcome your Son into my heart.
And I ask you to give me the grace, strength, and hope
to always live as your child,
with joy
and with love.
I raise my voice to you in prayer
during this, the greatest prayer on earth.

I pray for those I love,
knowing that you love them, too,
and want us, one day, to dwell with you
in eternal light.
Amen.

CHAPTER 9

YOU'VE GOT A FRIEND IN ME: THE PRAYER OF FRIENDSHIP

"This is my commandment: love one another as I love you. No one has greater love than this, to lay down one's life for one's friends."
—John 15:12-13

In the busyness of daily life, it can be easy not only to overlook God and prayer, but also to overlook, or even neglect, those who often give sustenance and support to our spiritual life: our friends.

We can take them for granted. We shouldn't.

It occurs to me that friendship itself can be a kind of prayer—an uplifting of the heart toward God. There is grace and goodness in companionship, support, solidarity. Being with another can be a celebration of God's creative work in the world.

I was reminded of this several years ago when I attended a monastic retreat with my friend Jeff—and we spent a lot more time talking than sitting in church praying.

At one point, the thought occurred to me: *Should I feel guilty?* The question nagged at me—a good Catholic question, pecking at my conscience as I sat under a shaggy tree on the grounds of a great monastery and listened to the bell as it tolled. It was time to pray. I should have been heading to the church. Others on retreat would be inside, under arches, chanting with the monks.

Instead, I was outside with Jeff, shooting the breeze, being decidedly non-contemplative. I should have been spending the day being silent, meditative, prayerful. Instead, I was yapping like a cocker spaniel. The bell was calling. I wasn't answering. I couldn't help but feel a twinge of guilt.

We had come to this remote place on a hot July weekend to share a little time, take a break, and catch up. Jeff and I attended Mass and a few of the liturgical offices. But mostly, we just hung out. I scanned the skies for birds. He smoked. We wandered the woods. He scribbled in his notebook. We griped about the Church and her scandals, and we marveled at the folly of humanity. We worried together, and laughed together, and solved the world's problems over gallons of black coffee, across a wooden table in the dining room or on two chairs on the retreat house porch.

The bell tolled. Ask not for whom. It tolled for me.

What kept me from going to the church? I have always been captivated by the offices of the monks—the chanting, the bowing, the hushed calm of men collected to pray. The psalms are part of that powerful experience, of course. Those 150 prose poems contain everything we need to know about life: it is glorious, it is horrible, it is maddening. And it goes on. The psalms are the human experience writ large. Out of the mouths of monks, they gain new resonance.

So why wasn't I joining them? What was I doing outside, swatting at flies?

I wondered about that and shrugged it off. Days later, at the end of our visit, as my plane climbed over the countryside and back to New York, I wondered something else. In spite of my frequent absences from church, why did I feel so surprisingly at peace?

What made me feel so—for want of a better word—graced?

I think I know. For all the riches of monastic prayer, there was another prayer that engaged me that weekend. It is a kind of everyday psalmody—found in a conversation, a laugh, a shrug, a nod. It is the prayer we all whisper at one time or another.

It is the simple liturgy of friends. For friendship, at its best, is a prayer.

It is, after all, an act of faith. It is sacred. It is an epistle, delivered from one person to another. In its best moments, friendship is a canticle that celebrates, a parable that teaches. In the close proximity of a friend, you find a cathedral where promises are kept, a chapel where tears are shed. Friendship is a responsorial psalm: one heart speaks, another responds, and in the silences in between, we hear something of God.

Jesus, no stranger to friendship—or to its swift reversal, betrayal—said that wherever two or more are gathered in his name, there he is too.

Finding Faith in One Another

Perhaps when we seek a friend, we are seeking God, the God who dwells in all of us, the God in whose image we have all been made. Perhaps in friendship he is there, waiting to be found—the God of laughter and companionship, the God of shared secrets, and long stories, and strong coffee, the God who is comfortable just kicking back. He is there to listen, because that's what friends are for. He is there to guide us on the journey, to see that we are not alone and that there is someone with us who can read the map. He is there to help us find faith in one another at moments when that particular faith may be all that we have. He is there to let us know that someone else understands our pain, shares our joy, and thankfully gets our jokes.

Out of that, we are encouraged and given hope. Out of that, I believe, we are given God.

There is something consoling, we know, in communal prayer. Hearts and voices join in one place, under one roof, at one moment in time, to acknowledge the Creator and ask his blessings. And in doing that, we acknowledge what we are—people bound by common faith, humility, and trust.

So it is, I think, in this extraordinary prayer of friendship.

With garden chairs as a choir, the lawn for an aisle, and the starry sky as a dome, my friend Jeff and I, on that summer weekend, prayed our own office, a private liturgy that bestowed on the two humble congregants a blessed amount of grace. The grace to be comfortable with another soul and feel a connection. The grace to enjoy the fading of twilight, or the stirring of leaves, or the simple silence that comes when

FRIENDSHIP, AT ITS BEST, IS A PRAYER. IT IS AN ACT OF FAITH. IT IS SACRED. IT IS AN EPISTLE, DELIVERED FROM ONE PERSON TO ANOTHER.

there is nothing really to say—and that's just fine too. Two or more were gathered.

And God, I believe, was there.

Unfortunately, I do not think you'll find that liturgy in any book of common prayer. It's not in the Roman Missal. Other rituals can be found there, beautiful testaments steeped in history and discipline. They are the handrails that guide us through the spiritual life. Without them we are lost.

But sometimes we find another way, on our own, and still manage to stumble upon God.

It is helpful, I think, to take time to offer the prayer of friendship. Consider it a kind of concelebration. A time for talking and listening, thinking and wondering. Kick back, open up, get another cup of coffee, crack a smile, heave a sigh—and listen.

You may hear, gently but surely, the happy beating of your own heart, like a bell tolling, quietly announcing that prayer has begun.

> The first man was not only created good, but was also established in friendship with his Creator.
>
> —*Catechism*, 374

> When Jesus speaks of his "friends," he points to a hard truth: true friendship involves an encounter that draws me so near to the other person that I give something of

my very self. Jesus says to his disciples: "No longer do I call you servants . . . but I have called you friends, for all that I have heard from my Father I have made known to you" (John 15:15). He thus establishes a new relationship between man and God, one that transcends the law and is grounded in trust and love. At the same time, Jesus frees friendship from sentimentalism and presents it to us as a responsibility that embraces our entire life: "Greater love has no man than this, that a man lay down his life for his friends" (15:13).

We become friends, then, only if our encounter is more than something outward or formal and becomes instead a way of sharing in the life of another person, an experience of compassion, a relationship that involves giving ourselves for others.

It is good for us to reflect on what friends do. They stand at our side, gently and tenderly, along our journey; they listen to us closely, and can see beyond mere words; they are merciful when faced with our faults; they are nonjudgmental. They are able to walk with us, helping us to feel joy in knowing that we are not alone. They do not always indulge us but, precisely because they love us, they honestly tell us when they disagree. They are there to pick us up whenever we fall.[18]

—Pope Francis

When you are with a friend, you are with God's creation—and, in fact, you are sharing part of your day with someone God has put into your life for a particular purpose. Appreciate the wonder of that. Cherish that person's presence in your life and your world. It is an unexpected blessing—companionship that is, in many ways, a gift of grace. Give thanks to God for the gift of that friend. Reflect on the meaning and purpose of that friendship—and look for God at work within it.

Dear God,
I give thanks to you for the gift of my friends.
You help me to remember I do not walk alone,
that you have given others to accompany me on life's journey.
May I always see you through others,
in others,
among others.
May you guide me closer to you
through them.
With these companions in my life,
may I be reminded of you,

the most cherished companion of all.
In their friendship,
may I see your friendship.
In their support, and encouragement, and laughter,
may I always see signs of your love.
And in moments when I feel uncertainty
or fear
or when I feel alone or unloved,
or abandoned by others,
help me to remember when your Son felt that way too.
Help me to know that you are with me,
that you love me,
and that you are always my Father
and my friend.
Amen.

CHAPTER 10

THE PRAYER OF FAMILY

Train the young in the way they should go;
even when old, they will not swerve from it.
—Proverbs 22:6

Honestly, I think one of the most overlooked and misunderstood Sundays on the Catholic calendar is the first Sunday after Christmas.

We've just about reached our fill. The turkey has become turkey salad. For the umpteenth time, we've told that distant cousin how much we love the handmade sweater she gave us that's two sizes too big and five shades of purple too ugly. (She's probably already making plans to make a matching scarf for next year.) The toys have run out of steam. Your uncle's dog has ruined the carpet. You've just about run out of jolly. And we've had about enough family for one year. When do the kids go back to school?

But it's right now, at this particular moment, that the Church gives us the feast of the Holy Family. It's Christianity's way of saying, "See? They did it. You can too."

This is the family that got it right.

And if we're going to consider some of the best practices to help busy people pray as a family, there's no better place to begin than with those three remarkable souls.

Jesus, Mary, and Joseph are continually held up to us as the great model of family life and family living. But who really can compete with a sinless virgin, the Son of God, and a quiet carpenter who, in all of Scripture, doesn't even utter a word? They seem so perfect—almost too perfect. Does that sound like any family you know? Our image of them isn't helped by the popular nativity scenes that pop up in churches and on Christmas cards: three well-groomed figures, frozen in permanent piety, halos in place.

The truth may have been quite different.

If we're going to think about and look toward the Holy Family as models of family prayer, it helps to understand this: they were a lot like us. They were holy, yes. But they were also human.

The story of the Holy Family is not just about perfection. Truth be told, it's the story of life not always turning out the way you planned. It's the story of a teenage girl conceiving a child she didn't expect, in a way she never imagined. (Think about it: she woke up one morning planning to live another typical day in Nazareth, running errands, doing chores, and whatever else young women did back then. She went to bed that night pregnant with the Messiah, yet still a virgin.)

It's the story of an anxious husband wrestling with doubt and questions—and even entertaining the possibility of divorce.

It's the story of an innocent child destined for martyrdom. Even in his infancy, a brutal dictator hunted him down and wanted him dead.

It's the story of a family displaced from their home, fleeing for their lives, living in the land that once held their ancestors as slaves. Whether or not they were, in fact, refugees—a category that some dispute—there's no disputing that they had to spend years in a foreign land, in a foreign culture, where their own ways of worship and their own belief in God were far different from those around them. They were, in every sense, strangers in a strange place—for all intents and purposes aliens.

So what can they teach us about prayer? A lot.

For all the difficulties they faced, all the struggles they endured, and all the hardships they confronted, this family also knew profound hope.

They trusted completely in God. And they call all of us to live with that kind of trust. And—this is what we cannot forget—they are with us.

In our own time, they stand beside all who worry, who struggle, who search, who pray.

The Holy Family stands beside parents anxious about their children, worrying about their welfare.

They walk with immigrants and refugees who are separated from those they love. They give companionship to those who feel isolated and alone.

They comfort teenage mothers and single parents.

They console prisoners and those condemned to die—and the parents who love them.

Look to the Holy Family, and you will find promise and possibility—and consolation. The Holy Family shares our burdens. But they also uplift us by their example. Jesus, Mary, and Joseph were never alone;

THE STORY OF THE HOLY FAMILY IS THE STORY OF LIFE NOT ALWAYS TURNING OUT THE WAY YOU PLANNED.

they endured through the grace of God. They prayed. They hoped. They trusted in God's will.

Where to Begin?

We might ask ourselves where we can find that kind of peace and purpose in our own families, in our own lives.

I think it begins by praying together. Father Patrick Peyton's familiar saying—"The family that prays together stays together"—really has the ring of truth. Beginning the practice of prayer together early and often can establish an ethic, set an example, and give direction and focus to any family, especially to the children.

In chapter 8, we considered the importance of the Mass in *your* life; let's take a look at it in the life of your family. Regular attendance at Mass can help build a weekly habit of devotion in the family, and help children grow accustomed to the "smells and bells," the traditions, the music, the vestments, the sense of ritual and of being in a sacred space. I know many parents who are reluctant to bring small ones to church because they can be fussy (or worse, noisy), and parents don't want to disrupt the Mass or distract the people in the pews. Once in a while I hear of parishes where other Mass goers are rude to these families or even cruel. (One typical comment: "Shouldn't you leave her at home until she's old enough to know what's going on?")

If you encounter problems or if you find your parish is less than supportive of small ones in the pews, take heart from this uplifting note I came upon at St. Thomas More Catholic

Church in Lynchburg, Virginia. I found these little advisories, along with crayons for coloring, at the entrance to the church when I visited a few years ago. I was happy to take a copy home and share it at my parish.

TO THE PARENTS OF OUR YOUNG CHILDREN, MAY WE SUGGEST . . .

- Relax! God put the wiggle in children. Don't feel you have to suppress it in God's house. All are welcome!

- Feel free to sit toward the front where it is easier for your little ones to see and hear.

- Quietly explain the parts of the Mass and actions of the priest, altar servers, choir, etc.

- Sing the hymns and pray and voice the responses. Children learn liturgical behavior by copying you.

- If you have to leave Mass with your child, feel free to do so, but please come back. As Jesus said, "Let the children come to me."

- Remember that the way we welcome children in church directly affects the way they respond to the Church, to God, and to one another. Let them know that they are at home in this house of worship.

- Please let your child use the reverse side of the card to draw and doodle.

TO THE MEMBERS OF OUR PARISH

- The presence of children is a gift to the Church! They are members of our community, and a reminder that our parish is growing. Please welcome our children and give a smile of encouragement to the parents.

On the back of the card were these words:

PEW ART

- Please let your child use this side of the card to draw and doodle. Take this with you as a reminder of your time in church.

Bringing your kids to Mass early and often can have other benefits too; you never know when the seeds of a vocation to the religious life might be planted.

Above and beyond churchgoing, the first "school of charity" remains the home. Gathering to pray every day as a family can only reinforce our love for one another and help us love our neighbors as well.

Family prayer need not take much time. A simple Sign of the Cross and short Our Father together at the start of every day can be enough. Grace before meals (see chapter 6) can encourage gratitude and humility. A prayer together at the end of the day (check out chapter 12)—maybe when tucking kids into bed—can foster a sense of devotion and even piety.

The important thing is to take a little time and make a little effort—this can make a tremendous difference. Regular, brief moments of prayer together as a family can give a sacred dimension to mundane moments and remind both children and parents that we exist for a greater purpose, to answer a higher call, to serve Someone beyond the confines of the world we know. We are here for God. And he is here for us.

Building on that idea and reinforcing it in daily life can help make a family whole and, by the grace of God, even holy.

> The home is the first school of Christian life . . . Here one learns endurance and the joy of work, fraternal love, generous—even repeated—forgiveness, and above all divine worship in prayer and the offering of one's life.
>
> —*Catechism*, 1657

I'm married, I have two children (ages thirteen and eleven), and I work. Life is busy and stressful. My main times for praying are on the subway during my morning commute, as a family before dinner, and at nighttime with the kids before they go to bed.

For as long as I can remember, I've always prayed to St. Anthony of Padua. (In fact, my son's middle name is Antonio.) When we say grace before dinner, we include a list of people who might need particular prayers—family members who are getting old, relatives and friends who are ill (too many people we know have cancer), plus our catchalls: 'All the souls in purgatory and anyone else who needs help.'

Before the kids go to bed, we say the Hail Mary in Italian, and we ask St. Anthony to pray for us and for our family and friends who need help. Taking time out to pray helps to keep me (somewhat) sane.

—JoAnn Longobardi, mother and lawyer,
Jamaica Hills, New York

Set aside a few minutes in the morning and a few more in the evening for regular family prayer. You might create a small worship space where parents and children can gather to pray before a crucifix or icon. Break open the Bible and ask someone to read a few verses. At mealtime, take a moment to pray grace together and express gratitude for what God has given your family. Offer special intentions when appropriate—remembering a family member or friend who may be in need of prayers. Heading out for a vacation? Before you go, gather for a short prayer for a safe journey—my parents always did this when I was growing up, and I never forgot it.

Make family prayer a frequent practice in the family, even if it's only for a few moments a day. You may be surprised at the impact it can have and the memories it can create.

Dear God,
We pray together as a family,
but also as your children.
May we always remember our bonds with each other
and with you:
bonds of loyalty and love,
bonds of forgiveness, and trust, and faith.
As we hold fast to your teaching and your truth,
help us to hold fast to each other.
Just as the Holy Family of Nazareth gave us a model,
may we continue to uplift each other,
support each other,
serve each other,
and help each other
to fulfill your plans and dreams for each of us.
Bless us with the quiet patience of Joseph,
the devoted obedience of Mary,
and the gentle humility of the baby Jesus.
Not just today,
but every day.
Amen.

CHAPTER 11

GOOD NIGHT, GOD

Even at night I remember your name
in observance of your law, LORD.
—Psalm 119:55

According to a popular saying that pops up on t-shirts and greeting cards, "A day hemmed in prayer seldom unravels."

Honestly, I've never been one to sew—I can barely attach a button to a shirt, let alone thread a needle or attempt anything more complicated—but this saying makes sense. When prayer begins the day, is threaded throughout the day, and sews it up at the end, life cannot help but feel whole. Awakening for God, living for him, cooking for him, cleaning for him, paying bills for him, driving for him, diapering for him, filing papers for him . . . it all works together, doesn't it?

So it is only natural that we would want to conclude the day with a word to the Almighty—in effect, a prayerful kiss good night.

Evening is the perfect time to reflect on the day just passed and, as the Catholic Confiteor (I Confess . . .) puts it, pray over "what I have done and . . . what I have failed to do."

The end of the day is also the perfect time to whisper a prayer of thanksgiving, grateful to God for all the blessings and abundant gifts of the day: the gift of work, the gift of home, the gift of friendship and family. It's also a time to recall those things that we often forget or neglect. Were there moments of laughter? Moments of joy? Were there small kindnesses offered by a coworker or a friend? Were there minutes, here and there, to quietly offer a prayer for another? Was this a day when we felt a special nearness to God—or when we felt that he made himself more present to us?

Do we take enough time to thank the Almighty simply for the gift of another day?

Evening prayer offers an opportunity to do that.

St. Ignatius of Loyola popularized one particular technique for prayer at evening, the Examen, or "examination." Many Jesuits and followers of Ignatian spirituality practice this a couple of times a day. There are plenty of online resources, books, and prayer guides to help you learn and practice it, too. For starters, the Jesuits' website (Jesuits.org) breaks it down into five basic parts:

1. **Place** yourself in God's presence. Give thanks for God's great love for you.

2. **Pray** for the grace to understand how God is acting in your life.

3. **Review** your day—recall specific moments and your feelings at the time.

4. **Reflect** on what you did, said, or thought in those instances. Were you drawing closer to God, or further away?

5. Look toward tomorrow—think of how you might collaborate more effectively with God's plan. Be specific, and conclude with the Our Father.

Fr. James Martin, the popular Jesuit author, puts it this way:

> Think of it as a movie playing in your head. Push the play button and run through your day, from start to finish, from your rising in the morning to preparing to go to bed at night. Notice what made you happy, what made you stressed, what confused you, what helped you to be more loving. Recall everything: sights, sounds, feelings, tastes, textures, conversations. Thoughts, words, and deeds, as Ignatius says. Each moment offers a window to where God has been in your day.[19]

What you find might not be what you hoped to find. You may remember some things you'd prefer to forget: along with the good, you'll find the bad and the ugly. You'll see more clearly, with immediate hindsight, "what I have done and what I have failed to do."

But there is grace in all of this. Praying over these moments at the end of the day can help us to redouble our efforts to do better tomorrow. By looking back on what was, we can be better prepared to look ahead to what will be.

We can get ready to begin again.

We can also make these last few sacred moments of wakefulness a silent prayer of petition to God who continues to watch over us, even while we sleep. Pray for resilience. Pray for reassurance. Pray for the courage to greet the next day with renewed zeal, piety, and hope. Pray for trust. Pray for those things you sense you need but cannot put into words.

Pray that God, who makes all things possible, will make possible another day, when he will again be present to you, walking with you, listening to you, and dreaming with you.

To Settle the Mind

The Liturgy of the Hours includes Night Prayer—you can easily say it in just a few moments. It offers an examination of conscience and the Confiteor, as well as a brief Scripture reading and some other short prayers. I find that praying Night Prayer helps settle my mind after a busy day and gives structure and a sense of conclusion to the day.

Finally, if you like to pray aloud, you can make that a daily practice at night too.

My wife and I conclude our day with a list of intentions. We pray for those we know who are sick, or unemployed, or anxious, or alone. Periodically, a parishioner or friend will ask us to pray for a special intention, and we'll do that too. We pray for those we remember—and even for those we forget to mention, because we know that God knows who they are.

The beauty and generosity of this simple act cannot be overstated. As our energy wanes, and the night deepens, and the darkness around us grows, we feel an inescapable connection to our brothers and sisters in need when we click off the lamp after prayer. We are reminded that we aren't alone. We hope and pray that those distant people we know (and a few we don't) will feel that connection too.

And we pray that God will watch over us all.

Out of energy? Out of time? The Lord's Prayer, followed by the timeless Night Prayer antiphon in the Liturgy of the Hours, can be a helpful end to any day:

> Protect us, Lord, as we stay awake;
> watch over us as we sleep,
> that awake, we may keep watch with Christ,
> and asleep, rest in his peace.

For a prayerful wrap-up after a particularly exhausting day, I'm also fond of this short, direct prayer by the first American-born saint, Elizabeth Seton: "Oh my God, forgive what I have been, correct what I am, and direct what I will be."

St. Elizabeth Seton's story is too astonishing to do justice to here. But her many roles in life—as a daughter of privilege, a wife, mother, widow, convert, and, finally, founder of the Sisters of Charity—make her a surprisingly effective witness when it comes to asking God for forgiveness and correction. If she can do it, anyone can!

PRAY FOR RESILIENCE. PRAY FOR REASSURANCE. PRAY FOR THE COURAGE TO GREET THE NEXT DAY WITH RENEWED ZEAL, PIETY, AND HOPE.

In fact, that very act of pleading for correction and forgiveness—and turning toward a new day—is fundamental, I think, to our Catholic Christian faith. It is intrinsic to the Sacrament of Reconciliation and also a vital building block for prayer. What could be a better way to end the day?

Try to keep that in mind as you click off the light, settle into the pillow, and prepare for a night's rest. Make this a moment not only for reflection but also for sincere and heartfelt prayer—a time for praise, for petition, for thanksgiving, and also for joyful hope. Who knows what God may have planned for the day yet to come?

Say, "Good night, God," and trust that he will make it so.

> May he support us all the day long, till the shades lengthen, and the evening comes, and the busy world is hushed, and the fever of life is over, and our work is done! Then in his mercy may he give us safe lodging, and a holy rest, and peace at the last.
>
> —Blessed John Henry Newman[20]

> My life as a human rights organizer concerning homelessness is a high-stress and fast-paced chaotic mixture of love, joy and inspiration . . . as well as stress, drama, and shamefully disgusting politics. I love my work, but I am cautious

because I have too often seen the stress of this work break people's spirit.

To maintain my spiritual sanity, I prioritize three things: I try to get out of the office and the seemingly endless meetings to spend time on the street and in homeless encampments to encounter the inspiring people on the margins who are Jesus in the flesh for me. I seek out spiritual direction and go to Confession regularly. And last, but extremely important, I make time to slip into a church to simply spend quiet time in the real presence of Christ in the Eucharist.

—Kelley Cutler, San Francisco, California

The Jesuit Examen is a good exercise for ending the day—but if that seems too daunting, take just five minutes to review the day. What were the high points? What were the low points? How can you do better tomorrow? Thank God for the blessing of the day, the gift of those around you, and ask the Lord to remain with you as you turn another page and prepare to face the world again. Close with the Our Father, and wish God a good night!

And if even that seems more than you can muster, you might remember these simple words of Pope St. John XXIII: "It's your Church, Lord. I'm going to bed."[21]

Dear God,
It is the end of another day,
and I conclude it as I began it:
alone here with only you.
You were with me at my first waking,
and I know you will be with me at the end of all my days.
Tonight I place my trust and hope again in you.
Thank you for the gift of another day—
its triumphs and trials, its joys and sorrows.
Thank you for another opportunity to walk with you
even though, so often, I stumble and fall.
Help me to get up and continue on.
Guide me on the right path.
Give me courage to be all you wish me to be,
and keep me safe through it all.
Amen.

CHAPTER 12

AMEN: HOW I PRAY

Let my prayer be incense before you;
my uplifted hands an evening offering.
—Psalm 141:2

By now, we're deep into the topic of how to make the practice of prayer a priority in our busy lives. But you may be thinking, "Easy for you to say, but how do *you* pray? Give us the specifics. What does your prayer look like day-to-day, not just on the subway or on retreat?"

Good question.

Can I change the subject?

Honestly, if I were looking for a model, an ideal, someone to single out as a fine example of piety and prayer, the last person I'd point to is myself. Prayer does not come naturally to me, and it isn't easy for me to find the time to pray either.

My days are jam-packed with meetings, deadlines, obligations, chores, projects, *stuff*. (I'm sure you can relate.) The alarm goes off at 6:00 a.m., I stagger out of bed at 6:30 (if I'm lucky), and I stumble toward the front door at 7:30 to make my way to the subway or the bus. Then, if I'm attentive, thoughtful, and not obsessed with some problem in my life, I make time to pray during the forty-five-minute commute to work.

I always carry two things in my shoulder bag: my iPhone and a copy of the monthly devotional *Give Us This Day* (full disclosure: I'm one of the contributing writers). I have the

Liturgy of the Hours on my iPhone (courtesy of iBreviary), so I'll begin my commute by praying Morning Prayer. If I have extra time, I like to dip into the Office of Readings and read the second reading. This is usually from an ancient Christian document—from one of the Fathers of the Church, for example—or is the work of various spiritual writers from later centuries. If I have any time left over, I'll read the daily reflection from *Give Us This Day*. More often than not, however, I'll save that for my evening commute home.

During the day, if I want a break, I'll check my iPhone and spend a few minutes with next Sunday's Scripture readings for Mass. One of my responsibilities as a deacon is to prepare a homily each week for Sunday Mass. I approach this task as a kind of *lectio divina*, the ancient Benedictine prayer practice whereby we meditate on Scripture as a kind of dialogue with the living word of God. I keep an eye out for recurring themes, words, phrases. I ask myself, "What do people need to hear from this? What do *I* need to hear? What message do I need to impart?"

ONE OF MY MOST PERSISTENT PRAYER PARTNERS OVER THE YEARS, PROVIDING BOTH INSPIRATION AND CONSOLATION, HAS BEEN MARY.

Whenever possible, I look for connections between the readings and modern life. I try to keep the readings in mind when I'm skimming the news—I check the headlines regularly for my blog, *The Deacon's Bench*—and I look for stories that surprise, inspire, move, or challenge me. The net effect is that homily preparation becomes an extension of my prayer time, and it challenges me to examine how well I'm measuring up to God's word. (Homily prep side tip: a great place to find interesting life lessons, even juicy quotes, is the obituaries. You'll sometimes find more miracles there than you can imagine.)

Mother of Mercy

Even when I am most alone, I have company in my prayer times. I have to say, one of my most persistent prayer partners over the years, providing both inspiration and consolation, has been Mary.

There *is* something about Mary. This humble woman, who unexpectedly found herself bearing the Messiah, reaches across time and space to offer us a continuing example of fidelity and trust. She is one of us, but her extraordinary faith sets her apart. She stands beside us, but she is also far above us. Somehow, she "let go and let God." Her life is a lesson to us all.

Caught in a jam? Suddenly dodging one of life's curve balls? Can't find the right words to pray in a moment of fear, desperation, or anxiety? We've all been there. Inevitably, in those moments, I find these words on my lips: "O Mary, conceived without sin, pray for us who have recourse to thee."

On my right wrist, I wear a plain brown rosary bracelet that has a bronze Miraculous Medal attached. When all else fails, this has become my go-to prayer resource. I've found that just one decade, even if whispered in worry or haste, can work wonders.

As I've learned again and again, Mary herself is a force to be reckoned with.

When I began studying to become a permanent deacon, a friend who is a magazine editor sent me a prayer card with an unusual depiction of the Blessed Mother.

"I think it's a good image for a writer," he told me. Well, I think it's a good image for anyone: a startling and altogether moving interpretation of the Mother of God.

William Hart McNichols, a Jesuit priest, is the artist, and he has titled the image *Mother of the Incarnate Word*. Mary is shown holding a book of Scripture in one hand, while touching her heart with the other. She is undeniably expecting: great with child, pregnant with possibility. The Word is both within and without—the truth that has been spoken, and the Truth still waiting to be heard. Mary is vehicle and vessel, pulpit and tabernacle.

Shortly after I received the card, I photocopied it and taped the copy inside my binder. And for the rest of my studies, Mary and the Word were there as I took notes, studied, read, and researched. The image became a symbol to me of the road I've traveled and the journey still ahead.

It was also a welcoming reminder of the consistent presence Mary has had in my own life—and in the lives of so many Catholics. To most of us, after all, the Mother of God is unavoidable. She is there in church corners and on side altars, a figure of wood or stone or plaster, hands folded in prayer, eyes gazing mercifully at all who kneel at her feet (which, depending on the interpretation, may be crushing a serpent or standing atop the moon). She is the Lady of Sorrows, the Queen of Martyrs, the Gate of Heaven, the Star of the Sea, the Immaculate Conception. Some know her as the Lady of Refuge, or the Seat of Wisdom, or the Pillar of Faith.

But to most of us, she is, quite simply, Mary.

I think that is probably how she prefers to be known. She was, after all, a simple woman. Full of grace, yes. But humble to her immaculate core.

And, like that image taped inside my binder, she has never been far from me.

Before I was born, my mother, having suffered three miscarriages and fearing a fourth, made a novena to Our Lady of the Miraculous Medal, praying that this child would somehow survive and be born. Well, I made it. And in ways large and small, Mary has been watching over me ever since.

Her name was on my lips as I learned one of my first prayers: "Hail Mary, full of grace." I remember long spring afternoons as a child, practicing for the May Procession, dozens of us lined up outside the church, flowers budding and bees buzzing as we sang, "Ave, ave, ave Ma-reeeeee-a" while clutching beads in our small hands.

As I got older, Mary remained a fixture in my life, through so many moments and milestones.

I don't think it's an accident that I was married at a chapel named for Mary, or that my bride's middle name is Marie, or that I was ordained at a basilica named for Our Lady of Perpetual Help, or that I now serve as a deacon at Our Lady Queen of Martyrs in a diocese whose patroness is Our Lady of the Immaculate Conception.

Mary has been keeping an eye on me.

And at the end of the day, after I've said the final words of Night Prayer, my wife and I take time to recite a prayer that was a favorite of my father's, the Memorare.

My father suffered a massive stroke that left him confined to a wheelchair and living in a nursing home for the last seven years of his life. He spent much of his waking hours praying this short verse—a plea that begins with one haunting word: "Remember."

> Remember, O most gracious Virgin Mary, that never was it known that anyone who fled to your protection, implored your help, or sought your intercession was left unaided. Inspired by this confidence, I fly unto you, O Virgin of virgins, my mother; to you do I come, before you I stand, sinful and sorrowful. O Mother of the Word Incarnate, despise not my petitions, but in your mercy hear and answer me.
> Amen.

My father died in 1990, but I pray this prayer daily for him, and with him, and for whatever intentions my wife and I might have. I know it helps me sleep better.

It brings me peace.

Indeed, at its deepest, most fundamental core, the act of prayer should be an act of peace—and one whose most immediate fruit is, in fact, peace. This straightforward communication with God—spoken with words from the heart—clears the mind, settles the soul, focuses the spirit, and serves as a replenishing balm. Prayer connects us with God and strengthens God's own connection with us.

The ancient word that concludes our prayer is thus an affirmation and a celebration: *Amen!* It says yes to all that we have prayed and yes to our faith and trust in the One to whom we have prayed. And nothing could be more enriching, uplifting, or peace building than that.

Isn't this what we all crave? Isn't that our deepest desire, as children of God and wandering souls, seeking salvation and an eternity in Paradise?

Yes. Amen.

> It is an old custom of the servants of God to have some little prayers ready and to be frequently darting them up to Heaven during the day, lifting their minds to God out of the mire of this world. He who adopts this plan will obtain great fruits with little pain.
>
> —St. Phillip Neri[22]

Prayer frames my day. Occasionally, I can do little more than pray, 'Good morning, dear Jesus; this day is for you, and I ask you to bless all I think, say, and do.' Stopping for ten minutes of silent prayer once, twice, or three times a day helps on a busy day, especially when I need to make a significant decision.

The goal of life is union with God. Prayer is a powerful, God-given means toward that goal. It also helps to teach me that every person, thing, and event, even at our busiest times, is a God-given means toward union with God.

—Rev. Bosco Peters, Christchurch, New Zealand

When all else fails, often the simplest and most straightforward prayer, whispered from the heart whenever you have a spare moment, can work wonders: "Dear God, give me hope." "Good God, help me find the words." "Father, be with me." A word to Mary can't hurt either: she can never ignore a plea from one of her children. "Mother Mary, pray for me" is often enough to still an anxious heart and afford a moment of peace.

Use free moments to offer a simple word of praise, gratitude, or hope to the One who makes all things possible. It will keep you connected to what really matters—and the Father who understands what we truly need.

Dear God,
Make me always willing to pray.
Make of my life a continual prayer:
a prayer of praise, of petition, of thanksgiving,
a prayer of hope.
Help me to be what you want me to be,
to give what you want me to give,
to serve as you want me to serve,
to love as you want me to love.
Make me desire nothing more or less
than to love you and to live for you.
That is my deepest longing
and my continual prayer.
Thank you for listening.
Amen.

CHAPTER 13

ONE MORE THING: SOME FINAL ADVICE

Prayer is like a secret garden made up of silence and rest and inwardness. But there are a thousand and one doors into this garden and we all have to find our own.

—Jean Vanier[23]

The high school I attended in suburban Maryland was named for St. Vincent Pallotti, the nineteenth-century saint who was the patron of the Second Vatican Council. Among other things, he was a great advocate for the laity in the life of the Church. In 1835, St. Vincent Pallotti founded the Union of Catholic Apostolate, a lay association that is considered a forerunner of Catholic Action. He described its mission this way:

> The Catholic Apostolate, that is, the universal apostolate, which is common to all classes of people, consists in doing all that one must and can do for the great glory of God and for one's own salvation and that of one's neighbor.[24]

He later expressed something that is central to all I have written in this little book: the idea that almost any aspect of our lives can be offered as prayer.

"You must be holy in the way God wants you to be holy," he said. "God does not ask you to be a Trappist Monk or a hermit. He wills that you sanctify your everyday life."[25]

This, I believe, is our great calling—and, in itself, a beautiful form of prayer.

As I was working on this book, I reached out to a woman who knows a lot about how to sanctify the everyday: Rose Sullivan. Known affectionately as "Mama Rose," she is the executive director of the National Conference of Diocesan Vocation Directors. She also happens to be the mother of a priest.

Rose is, as you can imagine, a busy person. She is also a woman of prayer. I asked her what ideas she could offer other busy people, from her many years of experience. What practical advice would she give?

She sent me the following email, and it summarizes perfectly what I consider the ideal prayerful ethic. Read on:

1. It may sound oversimplified, but try waking up just twenty minutes earlier, and give that time to God. It will be a game changer in starting your day—and you can even have your coffee while you are praying!
2. Driving to the seminary in the morning, I turn off the radio and turn on prayer time. My rosaries are never far from me, even if I only have time for a decade. Asking Mary, our most powerful intercessor, to guide us through our day and bring us ever closer to her Son is always an investment for the better for your soul.
3. You want your prayer to be a response to the presence and love of Jesus. Prayer is not a mix of some magical

words you recite that suddenly transports you into a deeper relationship with Christ. Prayer is a conversation with God. Take a coffee break; take a prayer break. Sometimes just stepping away from the joyful chaos of work and taking a quick break to walk, stretch, and reach out to God are all you need for that moment.

4. Pick up a good book on the saints, on Mary, on the Church; pick up the Bible, and just start reading.
5. Stop and simply invite God into the busyness of your day—"Jesus, be with me now." Although he always is with us, that quick prayer spoken throughout the day reminds us that he is, in fact, always there.
6. If you needed to get your child to soccer practice, had a deadline looming at work, and were preparing to welcome your relatives for a weekend stay, you would somehow get it all done. How? You make it work. How about putting God on that list? In fact, how about putting him on the top of your list? If you need to schedule your time to pray, then do it, and set a calendar notification.

At the end of the day, I think most of us can argue, perhaps defensively, that we are too busy to pray. How can we possibly do it? There's just too much going on!

"GOD WILLS THAT YOU SANCTIFY THE WORLD IN YOUR EVERYDAY LIFE."

But as my friend Rose reminds us: actually, we aren't too busy. Not at all.

The choice to pray is, fundamentally, a *choice*—just like the choice to read, or to cook, or to paint.

Or the choice to love.

Prayer is, after all, an expression of love. It is an expression of our abiding hope and faith in the God who made us and loves us—and of our own love for him.

And as an act of love—like any act of love—it is deeply rooted. It involves more than mere words.

Pope Francis has said,

> I . . . think of many Christians who think that praying is—pardon me—"talking to God like parrot." No! One prays from the heart, from within. . . . Our God needs nothing: in prayer he only asks that we keep a channel of communication open with him in order to always recognize that we are his most beloved children. He loves us very much.[26]

I submit that if we follow that path—praying from the heart, living each day as an ongoing prayer to the source of our joy and our hope—we can only draw closer to the One who desires that closeness forever.

Let us strive with confidence, faith, and trust to do that.

Let us strive to live that.

Let us pray.

APPENDIX

GOT A MINUTE? SAY A PRAYER
SOME SHORT, POPULAR CATHOLIC PRAYERS

The prayer most pleasing to God arises from a humble and loving heart . . . May each of us, personally, echo the plea of the disciples and ask, with great trust: "Lord, teach me to pray!"
—Pope Francis[27]

Beloved Pope St. John Paul II put it simply: "If you follow Jesus' advice, and pray to God constantly, then you will learn to pray well. God himself will teach you."[28]

Okay. We're willing to learn. So how can we start?

A good way to begin is to become familiar with some of the most popular and cherished Catholic prayers—the ones that mark our days, punctuate our liturgies, and define Catholic devotion around the world. These are prayers that remain both timely and timeless; you can pray them almost anytime and anywhere. Most are short and can be said in less than a minute.

Got a minute? God would love to hear from you.

The little compendium that follows is by no means definitive, let alone complete. But as I said, it's a start. Some of these prayers you may already know. Some may be buried somewhere in your memory—maybe a distant, fuzzy echo of what Sr. Margaret taught you in first grade. ("Hail Mary, something something something . . . Amen. I forget the rest.")

I hope this handy resource gives even the busiest person the tools to begin to pray.

Sign of the Cross

In the name of the Father
and of the Son
and of the Holy Spirit. Amen.

Our Father

Our Father, who art in heaven,
hallowed be thy name;
thy kingdom come;
thy will be done on earth as it is in heaven.
Give us this day our daily bread;
and forgive us our trespasses
as we forgive those who trespass against us;
and lead us not into temptation,
but deliver us from evil.
Amen.

Hail Mary

Hail Mary, full of grace, the Lord is with you;
blessed are you among women,
and blessed is the fruit of your womb, Jesus.
Holy Mary, Mother of God,
pray for us sinners,

now and at the hour of our death.
Amen.

Glory Be

Glory be to the Father, the Son, and the Holy Spirit;
as it was in the beginning, is now, and ever shall be,
world without end.
Amen.

Apostles Creed

I believe in God,
the Father Almighty,
Creator of heaven and earth;
and in Jesus Christ, his only Son, our Lord,
who was conceived by the Holy Spirit,
born of the Virgin Mary,
suffered under Pontius Pilate,
was crucified, died and was buried;
He descended into hell;
on the the third day he rose again from the dead;
he ascended into heaven,
and is seated at the right hand of God the Father almighty;
from there he shall come to judge the living and the dead.

I believe in the Holy Spirit,
the holy catholic Church,
the communion of saints,
the forgiveness of sins,

the resurrection of the body,
and life everlasting.
Amen.

Guardian Angel Prayer

Angel of God, my guardian dear,
to whom God's love commits me here,
ever this day be at my side,
to light and guard, to rule and
guide. Amen.

The Memorare

Remember, O most gracious Virgin Mary, that never was it known that anyone who fled to your protection, implored your help, or sought your intercession was left unaided.
Inspired by this confidence, I fly unto you, O Virgin of virgins, my Mother; to you do I come, before you I stand, sinful and sorrowful. O Mother of the Word Incarnate, despise not my petitions, but in your mercy hear and answer me. Amen.

Salve Regina (Hail, Holy Queen)

Hail, holy Queen, mother of mercy,
our life, our sweetness, and our hope.
To you do we cry, poor banished children of Eve;
to you do we send up our sighs,
mourning and weeping in this valley of tears.
Turn, then, most gracious advocate,
your eyes of mercy toward us;

and after this, our exile, show unto us
the blessed fruit of your womb, Jesus.
O clement, O loving, O sweet virgin Mary:
Pray for us, O Holy Mother of God,
That we may be made worthy of the promises of Christ.

Prayer of St. Francis of Assisi

Lord, make me an instrument of your peace;
Where there is hatred, let me sow love;
Where there is injury, pardon;
Where there is error, the truth;
Where there is doubt, faith;
Where there is despair, hope;
Where there is darkness, light; and
Where there is sadness, joy.
O, Divine Master,
grant that I may not so much seek to be consoled, as to console;
to be understood, as to understand;
to be loved as to love;
For it is in giving that we receive;
it is in pardoning that we are pardoned;
And it is in dying that we are born to eternal life.
Amen.

The Jesus Prayer

Lord Jesus Christ, Son of God, have mercy on me, a sinner.

Act of Contrition

My God, I am sorry for my sins with all my heart. In choosing to do wrong and failing to do good, I have sinned against you whom I should love above all things. I firmly intend, with your help, to do penance, to sin no more, and to avoid whatever leads me to sin. Our Savior Jesus Christ suffered and died for us. In his name, my God, have mercy.

ENDNOTES

1. Dr. Andrew Newburg, *NBC News*, "Power of Prayer: What Happens to Your Brain When You Pray?" accessed at https://www.nbcnews.com/news/religion/power-prayer-what-happens-your-brain-when-you-pray-n273956.

2. *Mother Teresa: Essential Writings*, Jean Maalouf, ed. (New York: Orbis Books, 2001).

3. St. Thérèse, *Manuscrits Autobiographiques*, as cited in the *Catechism of the Catholic Church*, 2558.

4. Patrick Burke, O Carm, "Interpreting Saint Teresa of Avila," http://www.carmelites.ie/InterpretingTeresa.pdf.

5. Pope John Paul II, Meeting with Young People of New Orleans, Apostolic Journey to the United States and Canada, September 12, 1987, 10, accessed at https://w2.vatican.va/content/john-paul-ii/en/speeches/1987/september/documents/hf_jp-ii_spe_19870912_giovani-new-orleans.pdf.

6. Brother Lawrence of the Resurrection, *The Practice of the Presence of God*, Conrad DeMeester, OCD, ed., Salvatore Sciurba, OCD, trans. (Washington, DC: ICS, 2015), 57.

7. Ibid.,125-126.

8. Brother Lawrence, *The Practice of the Presence of God*, Second Letter, accessed at http://prayerfoundation.org/booktexts/z_brother_lawrence_06.htm

9. Ibid., Seventh Letter, accessed at http:/prayerfoundation.org/booktexts/z_brother_lawrence_11.htm.

10. *Our Sunday Visitor Newsweekly*, "Gratitude," Mary DeTurris Poust, November 17, 2014, accessed at http://osvnews.com/2014/11/17/gratitude/

11. Pope Benedict XVI, General Audience, December 14, 2011, accessed at w2.vatican.va/content/benedict-xvi/en/audiences/2011/documents/hf_ben-xvi_aud_20111214.html.

12. Cardinal Robert Sarah, *The Power of Silence: Against the Dictatorship of Noise* (San Francisco: Ignatius, 2017), 23.

13. *The Guardian*, "One Blow after Another . . . and Finally Something Snapped," September 18, 2007, accessed at https://www.theguardian.com/books/2007/sep/18/classics.fscottfitzgerald.

14. Thomas Merton, *Thoughts In Solitude* (New York: Farrar, Straus, Giroux, 1999), 106.

15. Pope John Paul II, Address to the Young People of Bologna, 23rd Italian National Eucharistic Congress, September 27, 1997, 3, accessed at https://w2.vatican.va/content/john-paul-ii/en/speeches/1997/september/documents/hf_jp-ii_spe_19970927_youth-bologna.html.

16. Oscar Romero, *The Violence of Love*, trans. James R. Brockman, SJ (Farmington, PA: Plough, 2007), 42.

17. Sister Thea Bowman, interview, U.S. Catholic, cited here https://www.beliefnet.com/columnists/beyondblue/2010/07/let-me-live-until-i-die-an-int.html.

18. Pope Francis, Address to the 75th Convention of Serra International, June 23, 2017, accessed at w2.vatican.va/content/Francesco/en/speeches/2017/June/documents/papa-francesco_20170623_convention-serrainternational.html.

19. James Martin, SJ, *The Jesuit Guide to (Almost) Everything: A Spirituality for Real Life* (San Francisco: HarperOne, 2012), 91.

20. John Henry Newman, Sermon 20, accessed at http://www.newmanreader.org/works/subjects/sermon20.html.

21. Cardinal Timothy M. Dolan, *Priests for the Third Millennium* (Huntington, IN: Our Sunday Visitor, 2000).

22. Jill Haak Adels, *The Wisdom of the Saints: An Anthology* (New York: Oxford University Press, 1987), 39.

23. Jean Vanier, *Community and Growth,* Ann Shearer, trans. (New York: Paulist, 1989), 190.

24. Union of Catholic Apostolate, accessed at https://www.unionofcatholicapostolate.org/.

25. *Pallottine Renewal Center Blog*, accessed at https://pallottinerenewalblogdotorg.wordpress.com/.

26. Pope Francis, General Audience, January 2, 2019, accessed at http://w2.vatican.va/content/Francesco/en/audiences/2019/documents/papa-francesco_20190102_udienza-generale.html.

27. Pope Francis, General Audience, December 5, 2018, accessed at https://www.romereports.com/en/2018/12/05/pope-francis-begins-new-catechesis-on-the-lords-prayer-in-general-audience/.

28. Pope John Paul II, Address, Apostolic Journey to the United States and Canada, Meeting with the Young People of New Orleans, September 12, 1987, accessed at https://w2.vatican.va/content/john-paul-ii/en/speeches/1987/september/documents/hf_jp-ii_spe_19870912_giovani-new-orleans.html.

Acknowledgments

I owe a profound debt of gratitude to many people who have made this book possible—and made working on it so fulfilling!

First, my deepest thanks go to the good people at The Word Among Us Press, who first approached me with the idea for this book. Evidently someone thought, *Who's the busiest person we can think of to write a book for busy people?* And here I am.

Beth McNamara, born with the patience of a saint (or at least that of a very kindly and sympathetic editor), nudged me along as needed and provided periodic pep talks. She didn't even flinch when I told her, "You know that deadline I had in September? I'm not going to make it." Thank you, Beth, for not killing me.

A grateful diaconal bow also to Cynthia Cavnar, an editorial wizard who somehow made sense of what often seemed senseless and who managed to be savvy, and sane, and wonderfully supportive.

I couldn't have completed this endeavor without some accomplices—including a number of friends, contacts, colleagues, and friends of friends who lent their thoughts, ideas, prayers, and time. Some asked innocently, "How's the book going?" and then listened politely as I broke into sobs; they just quietly passed me a Kleenex box so I could blow my nose and dry my eyes. Others went above and beyond the call of duty (and friendship) and contributed the brief reflections on prayer that close most chapters. I'm blessed to know so many busy, thoughtful, prayerful people. Thank you, thank you.

I'm also thankful to the friends God has placed around me. Earlier, I mentioned that friendship is a prayer. The abiding, lived prayer of so many made writing about prayer a joy. These are people who have inspired me, consoled me, nudged me, and uplifted me—including my parishioners and friends at Our Lady Queen of Martyrs Catholic Church in Queens, my colleagues at Catholic Near East Welfare Association (CNEWA), Aleteia, and Patheos (I'm looking at you, Elizabeth Scalia) and my family in Maryland, especially my sister Karen. You all have prayed for me, and prayed with me, as I have prayed for you, and you have helped me understand more deeply the power of prayer to work wonders—even to bring about the birth of a new book. I'm in awe.

Finally, I can only offer a lifetime of love and thankfulness to my wife, Siobhain, whose fingers have worn out so many rosary beads and whose lips have whispered "Aves" for her husband again and again and again for thousands of reasons, large and small, across nearly forty years of friendship, marriage, headaches, job changes, mortgage payments, sleepless nights, deacon classes, preaching commitments, out of town retreats, parish missions and, of course, love. I couldn't have done it without you. You've proved again and again that prayer works, even among the busiest people. Thank you for that and so much more.

ABOUT THE AUTHOR

Deacon Greg Kandra is the creator of the blog *The Deacon's Bench,* carried on the popular website Patheos. The blog has garnered some 20 million readers from around the world since its inception in 2007. Additionally, he serves as the multimedia editor for Catholic Near East Welfare Association (CNEWA), a pontifical association founded by Pope Pius XI in 1926. He oversees the agency's blog, *One-to-One,* and is one of the editors of its award-winning magazine, *ONE.*

Before joining CNEWA, Deacon Greg spent nearly three decades in broadcast journalism, most of that time at CBS News, where he was a writer and producer for several programs including *48 Hours, 60 Minutes II, Sunday Morning,* and *The CBS Evening News with Katie Couric.* He was also the founding editor of *Couric & Co.,* Katie Couric's blog at cbsnews.com. In addition to his work with CBS News, from 2000 to 2004, he served as a writer and producer on the live finales of the hit reality series *Survivor.*

In 2002, he cowrote the acclaimed CBS documentary *9/11,* hosted by Robert DeNiro, which told the story of firefighters on September 11, 2001. The film showed the only footage shot inside the World Trade Center that day and featured the last images of Fr. Mychal Judge, moments before he became the first official fatality of the attacks.

In print, Deacon Greg's radio essays were featured in Dan Rather's best-selling book *Deadlines and Datelines*. His essays have been published in *America, U.S. Catholic, Catholic Digest, Reality,* and the *Brooklyn Tablet*. He also contributes reflections to *Give Us This Day*, the monthly prayer periodical from Liturgical Press. In the fall of 2018, Ave Maria Press published his first book, *The Living Gospel: Daily Devotions for Advent 2018*.

Deacon Greg has received every major award in broadcasting—including two Emmys, two Peabody Awards, and four awards from the Writer's Guild of America. His spiritual writing and essays have been honored multiple times with awards by the Catholic Press Association. He's one of seventy-six New Yorkers—including Dorothy Day and Fulton Sheen—profiled in the 2014 book *New York Catholics*.

Deacon Greg travels the country directing retreats and parish missions. In May 2016, at the invitation of the Vatican, he was one of the featured speakers at the international Jubilee for Deacons in Rome. In 2017, he became the first deacon to be honored as Clergy of the Year by the Catholic Guild at Our Lady of the Skies Chapel at John F. Kennedy Airport. He was one of the speakers at the 2018 Diaconate Congress in New Orleans, marking the fiftieth anniversary of the restoration of the diaconate as a permanent order.

A Maryland native, Deacon Greg graduated from the University of Maryland with a BA in English in 1982. He was ordained a deacon for the Diocese of Brooklyn in 2007. He and his wife live in Forest Hills, New York, where he serves at Our Lady Queen of Martyrs Parish.